THE NONTOXIC CEO

PROTECTING YOUR PEOPLE, PLANET, AND PROFITS
THROUGH BETTER CHEMICAL MANAGEMENT

THE NONTOXIC CEO

PROTECTING YOUR PEOPLE, PLANET, AND PROFITS
THROUGH BETTER CHEMICAL MANAGEMENT

A Road Map to 21st Century Corporate Responsibility

MARK WYSONG

Beyond Words Publishing, Inc.
20827 N.W. Cornell Road, Suite 500
Hillsboro, Oregon 97124-9808
503-531-8700

Design: Overland Agency, Inc.

Printed in the United States of America
Distributed to the book trade by Publishers Group West

Library of Congress Cataloging-in-Publication Data

Wysong, Mark L.
   The Nontoxic CEO: protecting your people, planet, and profits through better chemical management / Mark Wysong.—1st ed.
      p. cm.
   Includes bibliographical references.
   ISBN 1-58270-105-9
      1. Industrial management—Environmental aspects. 2. Industrial management.
      3. Hazardous substances—Management. 4. Environmental responsibility. I. Title.
HD30.255.W96 2003
658.4'08—dc21   2003012550

The corporate mission of Beyond Words Publishing, Inc.:
   Inspire to Integrity

CONTENTS

ACKNOWLEDGEMENTS

First I credit Mr. Greg Tozian (Overland Agency, Portland, Oregon) for the challenge that compelled me to extract from mind, share, and commit to paper the concepts of Compliance-Side Total Chemical Management (CSTCM). Greg's commitment and tireless persistence proved vital to the initiation and completion of *The Nontoxic CEO*.

I consider myself blessed to have worked day in and day out for the last twelve years with Ms. Debbie Sepich and Dr. Tim Doré. These cofounders, co-laborers, co-contributors have allowed me the rare privilege to dream and lead from a position of vision. As the CSTCM vision took form, these two made sure both my feet were planted and grounded in reality. Their ability to understand and implement real-world chemical management solutions provided the baseline for critical CSTCM principles. With their help, we identified patterns of chemical management and value recovery opportunities in over one hundred companies. Hopefully your company will be next.

Others have made various contributions to *The Nontoxic CEO*. Mike Butler, Dave Karstens, and Mark Heins all contributed to the aggregation and interpretation of terabyte buckets of chemical data. Scott Towsey audited our model assumptions and provided inclusive analysis tools that help define CSTCM value. I am indebted to each of you.

My wife, Kelley, and my daughter, Ashley, provided unwavering support during the long nights and weekends spent writing the first draft. This literary birthing process proved longer and more time-consuming than anyone could have predicted, and I thank them. Thanks also to Denise, Angie, and Joy for their confidence and belief in their father.

Finally, my deepest respect and gratitude to all EH&S, Toxicology, Industrial Hygiene, IT, and Senior Management Professionals who have dared to bring Best Practices to their companies' Chemical Compliance Programs. I count many of you among my closest friends and all of you have enriched my life! It is for you that this book is written.

WHAT IS A "NONTOXIC" CEO?

In the course of working on this project, when I told people that I was writing a business book titled *The Nontoxic CEO*, most of them invariably got a smile on their faces and responded by asking me one of two questions. If they happened to work at one of the companies in the United Sates that use hazardous chemicals, they'd say, "Oh, you mean it's something to do with corporations using fewer toxic chemicals?"

"Yes," I would say, "that's right! That is part of it."

If they didn't work at one of these companies, they'd ask, "You mean as in learning how to become a better boss?"

"Yes," I would say, "that's right! That is part of it."

Both questions are valid, and both answers are partly right.

For the purposes of this guide to a new kind of corporate responsibility, becoming a nontoxic CEO (or nontoxic Senior VP, or Health & Safety Officer, or nontoxic anything else in your company) will definitely require that you manage your hazardous chemicals more responsibly.

"Nontoxic" in this sense does not mean you do away with all hazardous chemicals. That's not practical. You'll do away with some chemicals, however, and the rewards of a nontoxic approach to management will pay you back tenfold in a variety of important ways. For one, you will give increased protection to your workers, your environment, and your bottom line by learning how to use fewer hazardous chemicals and better manage the ones you do keep. This brand of nontoxic management is Compliance-Side Total Chemical Management, or simply CSTCM™. It's a concept that dovetails nicely into your existing risk-management programs. And what are the rewards? Plenty. In this book, you'll read about:

- A forest products company that enjoyed a healthy 70 percent reduction in chemical inventories, which saved and is saving the company millions of dollars

- A utility now working with CSTCM that stands to save $10 million each year, thanks to a 50 percent reduction of its inefficiently purchased, stored, and potentially dangerous chemical inventory

- Other industry profiles showing a range of real-life companies with big annual savings since they began managing their chemicals better with CSTCM

One of the best parts of CSTCM is that it works through the existing government-mandated compliance machinery that is already in any American company that deals with hazardous chemicals (that's millions of companies!). CSTCM is also very democratic, since no matter how large or small your company, or how many locations or employees you have, it will help you better protect your people, planet, and profits. Being a nontoxic CEO also includes becoming a better boss. That's a plus that I'm sure you will appreciate. Values, both the do-the-right-thing kind and the economic variety, are what this book is all about.

As you follow the advice in this book, you will learn how to practice a form of integrated management that will require getting a lot of people to pull together to make a big difference. That integrated, people-matter approach to management will naturally make you shine. When you do nontoxic leadership correctly, look at what you can accomplish:

- Your employees will feel (and be) safer
- Everyone at your company will be proud of your environmental contributions
- Your public relations people will have something positive to crow about
- The public may think more highly about you
- Your shareholders will love the return on their investment
- And you'll have a right to feel like you are a "better boss"

About now, you may be asking, "If being a nontoxic CEO is so great, why isn't everybody who deals with chemicals nontoxic?" As you will see from the numerous citations and case studies that follow, there are plenty of companies practicing better chemical management and there are more than a few nontoxic CEOs already in existence. But there are more of your peers who are toxic and don't even know it! And it's the not knowing part that is the most dangerous.

When it comes to nontoxic leadership, as with any paradigm shift, learning how to be a nontoxic CEO requires new ways of thinking and more efficient methods of resource management. Promotion and salesmanship are also involved in implementing a successful program of better, or total, chemical management. People will have to think and act in bold new ways. You'll need corporate champions and lots of guts. As the saying goes, "No guts, no glory." And let me tell you, being nontoxic is glorious.

So what are you waiting for? Your employees, vendors, customers, and shareholders are all counting on you to do the right thing, socially and financially. Your curiosity and desire have brought you this far; the next step to becoming a nontoxic CEO is turning the page.

SECTION 1

BECOMING NONTOXIC

PROTECTING YOUR PEOPLE, PLANET, AND PROFITS

You May Already Be Toxic!

There are perhaps several million toxic CEOs in America today who are unwittingly operating their companies in various degrees of toxicity, blissfully unaware of all the harm it could mean for their people, planet, and profits. Are you a toxic CEO or other toxic company employee? Before you answer that question with, "No, of course not!" take a few minutes to read on and really find out.

The several million toxic CEOs are the heads of companies that deal—not as well as they could—in some way and on a regular basis with one or more of what the Occupational Safety and Health Administration (OSHA) estimates are 650,000 hazardous chemicals used today in three million American workplaces. These companies, like the chemicals they use, are simply everywhere; they are part of our industrialized, highly technological present—and future. It is almost easier to list the industries that do not use hazardous chemicals than those that do. In Figure 1, you will find an eye-opening list of industry sectors that deal regularly with large volumes of hazardous chemicals.

By referring to CEOs and companies as "toxic," I am being metaphorical. America's plentiful toxic leaders aren't doing anything so blatantly wrong as to present a significant danger to their workers, the environment, and their bottom line. But most of these corporate over-seers could be managing their hazardous chemicals better. All of them could reduce the number and volume of hazardous substances their organizations handle and dispose of, to the benefit of their social responsibility and financial returns.

Our modern world clearly needs hazardous chemicals for critical manufacturing and sometimes life-saving processes. But as hazardous chemicals and other dangerous materials are identified as unacceptably damaging to people and the planet, they must go. I am a firm believer

FIGURE 1.

U.S. sectors that deal regularly with large volumes of hazardous chemicals:

- Pharmaceutical and health care
- Automotive and robotics-automation
- Forest, pulp, and paper products
- Semiconductors and other high-tech manufacturing
- Health and beauty
- Chemical and petroleum manufacturing
- Laboratory sciences
- Home-building and industrial materials
- Furniture production
- Utilities and telecommunications
- Printing and graphics
- Aviation and other transportation providers
- Engineering and agriculture
- Large chain retail operations
- Apparel manufacturing and packaging
- Photography and entertainment
- Food and beverage processing
- Construction and contracting
- Hotels and lodging
- Home electronics and consumer products manufacturing

that chemicals have added immeasurably to the quality and length of our lives on this planet; however, it is imperative that you—as a non-toxic CEO—learn to manage your chemicals as responsibly as you can.

In subsequent chapters, I will outline a new management paradigm—I call it Compliance-Side Total Chemical Management (CSTCM). This systematic approach will bring measurable results in better chemical management and financial benefits to the huge niche of businesses that deal with hazardous chemicals on a regular basis.

U.S. industries now spend tens of billions of dollars a year to comply with government-mandated Environmental Health and Safety (EHS) regulations. OSHA requires companies to have a Material Safety Data Sheet (MSDS) for anything that is hazardous, so that workers know how to use chemicals safely. It often seems, judging by the millions of MSDSs in existence, that everything is hazardous! Yet, through better chemical management, reducing the number and volume of hazardous chemicals in use, companies also save a great deal of money. These companies simultaneously reduce their financial risk in terms of penalties, costly cleanups, and litigation.

For those of you who like to cut to the chase, I direct your attention to a couple of particularly impressive case studies that illustrate the financial (as well as safety and environmental) returns of CSTCM. In chapter 1 (*Why You Need CSTCM*), you will read about a world-leading manufacturing company that literally cleaned up its hazardous-chemicals act after a devastatingly expensive chemical disposal *faux pas*. In the same chapter you'll also read about a utility that is moving toward saving millions, year after year, by reducing its chemicals—hazardous and otherwise—through simple CSTCM solutions.

A WORD ABOUT TOTAL CHEMICAL MANAGEMENT

Total Chemical Management (TCM) is not a new concept. Dozens of U.S. companies have been reaping financial benefits for a decade or more by reducing their chemical count and volume, substituting products, implementing operational and process changes, and even green-engineering cleaner products.

If you decide to investigate and eventually adopt a TCM program, you will be in good company. Leading corporations that have benefited from some form of TCM in recent years include 3M, DaimlerChrysler, Delta Air Lines, DuPont Chemical, Dow Chemical, Ford Motor Company, General Dynamics Corp., General Motors (GM), General Electric, Harley Davidson, Hewlett-Packard, Honeywell, IBM, Motorola, Navistar, Nortel Networks, Northwest Airlines, Novartis, Nu-Metal Finishing, Raytheon, Seagate Technologies, Texas Instruments, and United Technologies.

The system advocated in this book, however, is a fairly new and par-ticularly democratic solution. Unlike the TCM of the past, which is prejudiced in favor of large-volume users of chemicals, CSTCM has worked well for some big, chemically intense companies, but it proves to work just as well for small and mid-sized operations. That's because CSTCM approaches savings through EHS compliance machinery, which any company that uses hazardous chemicals already has in place in some form by government mandate. Since you already employ a person (or whole departments of people) responsible for complying with government regulations, why not use your compliance motion to recapture some of your hard-earned dollars? This book's goal is to teach you how to turn compliance pain into compliance profits.

If you are one of our country's toxic CEOs and you do not know that you are, it's not the end of the world. Then again, it might be the end of your career if you are a corporate leader on the receiving end of an accidental toxic release or outright disaster that harms your people or the environment. In fact, your professional downfall might just as easily occur as the result of a large state or federal financial penalty and resulting negative publicity for some transgression of the regulations governing hazardous chemical handling and disposal. Such a mishap—whether physically or financially devastating—may quickly erode your stakeholders' (including employees, vendors, shareholders, customers, and the media) esteem and confidence in you and your company. Either way, you'll be history—just another toxic statistic.

This book consists of two parts. CEOs and VPs of EHS will be most interested in section 1, which deals directly with the corporate vision needed to implement a successful CSTCM program. Section 2 is a nuts-and-bolts approach that will show the implementers of

CSTCM—whether they are EHS specialists, toxicologists, or IT people—how to go about fulfilling their part of the process. This section serves as a road map for implementing a largely painless and rewarding program of better chemical management that is well worth the effort.

This book will lead you through a new way of dealing with purchasing (and reducing) hazardous chemicals in your business—whether your operations entail just one site or an enterprise-wide system with hundreds of locations. This book will also show you how to build a business case for better chemical management, look at and audit your current system, implement alternatives, measure your success and maintain it, and even how to properly tell your shareholders and the world-at-large your success story.

Before I begin to guide you on the path to becoming a nontoxic CEO, I will admit that I am biased in believing in the honesty, good intentions, and competence of the corporate leaders with whom I work. Over the past dozen years my company has been a service provider for more than one thousand businesses, including many Fortune 500 entities. This amounts to a large group of of reputable, well-intended, and talented individuals.

Before diving into the how-to you will need, I would like to provide some context for the terms "nontoxic CEO" and "better chemical management." What is *bad* chemical management? What makes it so bad? How have American companies arrived where they are today vis-à-vis hazardous substances, human health and safety, and environmental regulations? You should already be familiar with state-of-the-art concepts such as "corporate responsibility" and "corporate sustainability," they are buzz phrases for 21st century business.

CEOS ARE UNDER THE GUN

As we sit at the helm of our government-regulated businesses, helping to steer the world's leading nation into the unknown challenges of the 21st century, is there a more maligned job title on this planet than that of CEO?

With numbing regularity, network news agencies air special reports on corporate irresponsibility. Enron's missteps have given business leaders in countless, completely unrelated industries a black eye. Meanwhile, the more excitable World Trade Organization (WTO) opponents and more strident environmentalists assure us that the world is going to hell in a handbasket—and I don't have to tell you who they believe is carrying the basket.

Such Chicken Little-like prognostications of the earth's eminent environmental collapse might invite one to paraphrase Mark Twain's quip about premature public reports of his death: they are "greatly exaggerated." If we are careful about the way we approach our 21st century business and social consciousness, our planet will be fine. But a healthy world needs constant and careful maintenance. That means CEOs, VPs of EHS, their employees, and vendors must build a safer planet through nontoxic thinking and doing.

There are, of course, a number of CEOs out there who are shining examples for others. All of us in the business world know, have read about, and have seen in the media the kinds of CEOs who serve as great role models for the rest of us. As I was entering the editing stage of this book, the magazine *Safety + Health* ran "CEOs Who 'Get It'" as its February 2003 cover story. The magazine's editors singled out the CEOs of such companies as Delphi Corp., Miller Brewing Co., United Parcel Service (UPS), and Home Depot as among the best in the nation for ensuring worker safety. The editors also laid the reason behind CEOs doing the right thing on the doorstep of values. "Values represent what are truly important to a company and speak to expectations about how the company and its employees should behave," the editor wrote.

I couldn't agree more. In the final analysis, "values" are really what this book is about. Throughout the book, you will read about the benefits that CSTCM will bring your company. But if you, as a corporate leader, and your CSTCM team aren't inspired to greater human and environmental health through a value system that is wedded to your corporate culture, I can't imagine you will be truly successful in the long run.

LEADERSHIP IS TOUGH

In considering the current, very real problems of CEOs, I gained some insights from Jeffrey E. Garten's excellent book, *The Mind of the C.E.O.* (Perseus Publishing, 2001). Garten, Dean of the Yale School of Management, identifies three major challenges for today's CEOs: 1) dealing with the Internet and the global economy, 2) dealing with daily operational challenges, and 3) delivering on increasingly important demands for corporate social responsibility. Garten concludes that where CEOs fail the worst is on the third challenge: social responsibility. This is due to the main problems of "toxicity" that I see in CEOs of even small and mid-sized companies.

We are rapidly reaching a day in America—and the world-at-large—where corporate responsibility will feel less and less optional. Shareholders, the media, employees, and private citizens will all want to know what you are doing to protect your people, planet, and profits. Why not get ahead of the curve? CSTCM is one way you can make a difference in all three categories.

HAVING VISION IS TOUGHER

What is helping make—and keep—our nation's toxic CEOs toxic in the first place is one of the sobering laws of human kind: *the single greatest deterrent for doing the right thing is a lack of vision.* An observation that perfectly illustrates this point comes from one of the great minds of the last century: Albert Einstein. The great mathematician told a biographer, "I know why there are so many people who love chopping wood. In this activity, one immediately sees the results."

What too frequently prevents perfectly adequate companies (meaning the majority of business ventures) from becoming truly leading and great operations is that their CEOs (and other vision leaders) often focus too much on merely chopping wood—going after those immediate results. Garten refers to this as focusing on the bottom line to the detriment of responsibility.

It's true that short-term results can be very gratifying, and profitable. But it's also true that you can get results that are even more rewarding by following a slightly different vision and planning just a little more time for even better results. The business community has witnessed a series of fast-evolving new management paradigms that require greater investments of time, money and teamwork, but undeniably yield incredible benefits. You know what I'm talking about: the Five Rings, Total Quality Management, Six Sigma, and ISO programs.

Accordingly, this new management paradigm of CSTCM will take vision, guts, and commitment, but it can bring you measurable results if your business uses a lot of hazardous chemicals.

TOXIC CEOS ARE UNDER A BIGGER GUN

How uncomplicated the days before the invention of hazardous chemicals seem! U.S. manufacturers faced little or no challenge managing the few, simple, hazardous substances present in 1802 when DuPont began to produce gunpowder in a little shack beside a quiet Delaware creek.

To the basic soda ash, alkalis, and dyestuffs that DuPont and other early chemical companies employed in the 19th century, complexity reared its head with the addition of synthetic ammonias and fibers. Then came plastics, polymers, and resins. The chemical industry in the U.S. skyrocketed tenfold, from a mere $150 million tadpole in 1880 to a $1.5 billion giant thirty years later. As the Industrial Revolution kicked into high gear (particularly after World War I), oceans of chemicals began flooding the U.S. marketplace. Our lives are now immeasurably better because of modern chemicals, but we have seriously increased the dangers of dealing with new hazardous materials and their wastes.

Today more than 25,000 chemical manufacturers in the U.S. represent a $464 billion industry. Chemicals are so important to our way of life that they represent the largest U.S. export and a quarter of the world's production, according to the American Chemistry Council. One out of every seven patents issued in the U.S. is chemical related. American business manufacturing operations use chemicals to produce an estimated 70,000-plus products including clothing, medicines, fertilizers, foods, detergents, packaging materials, paints, adhesives, fuels, furniture, tires, automobile parts, aircraft composite materials, computer microprocessors, spacecraft equipment, building materials, and myriad other staples of modern living.

But for every one of those 70,000 products, there are many people concerned about what American business is creating, using, and disposing of in terms of hazardous chemicals. As a CEO whose company deals with toxics, you are fair game for anyone interested in the human and environmental threats your chemicals conceivably pose. Of course you will always have to be conscious of the media's interest in your environmental performance. In the words of one senior proactive environmental risk-management manager I consulted, "If my boss reads about it in the *Wall Street Journal*, I've failed!"

But it is not simply the media with whom you must maintain a reputation for responsible chemical management. You already know about OSHA and the Environmental Protection Agency (EPA) and their state equivalents that regulate your dealings with chemicals. Now add to their scrutiny dozens of nonprofit watchdog organizations. Chief among these are such groups as Greenpeace, Sierra Club, the national and highly vocal CorpWatch, well-funded environmental lobbies such as Public Citizen and Essential Information, the National Coalition Against the Misuse of Pesticides, the Natural Resources Defense Council, Friends of the Earth, the World Wildlife Fund, and Mothers and Others for a Livable Planet. You may also have very aggressive statewide organizations watching and reporting further on what you do with hazardous chemicals, such as New York's Toxics Targeting group (which "tracks 400,000 known and potential toxic sites, including abandoned landfills, leaking tanks, hazardous waste generators and pollution discharges to air, land, or water"), and the well-organized Washington Toxics Coalition.

Adding to your company's life under the microscope is the proliferation of industrial information on the Internet, including the publication of the EPA's Toxic Release Inventory (TRI) and the Environmental Defense Fund (whose *Scorecard* website gives private citizens nationally "the facts on local pollution.")

What all of this means is that literally any private citizen with Internet access—whether or not they live near any of your facilities that report toxic releases—can obtain and confront you with information specific to your chemical usage. In chapter 3 (*Telling the World Your Success Story*), I will discuss at greater length how and why it is so important that you tell your story correctly when you share your chemical management victories with the media and the public. Ultimately, it is the nation's CEOs who must answer to their stakeholders everywhere about the myriad hazardous chemicals used in industry today. With all the wonders of modern living and the prosperity chemicals have brought to our lives, your challenge as a nontoxic CEO is to manage your chemicals better and reduce hazardous chemicals where you can.

MANAGING CHEMICALS IS DANGEROUS

To state the obvious, the reason so many people in America (and throughout the industrialized world) are so interested in hazardous chemicals is because these substances are dangerous. Perhaps those dangers are most clearly understandable by looking at some of the catastrophic chemical-related events that executives have had to face in recent memory. These events shook some large American companies to their foundations.

- In 1977 residents of a small upstate New York area began complaining about strange, apparently toxic substances oozing into their basements. After two years of federal emergencies, government cleanups, and the relocation of hundreds of people, it was determined that a local company had abandoned 20,000 tons of toxic chemicals in nearby Love Canal. After 16 years of battling a Justice Department lawsuit, in 1995 Occident Chemical Corporation agreed to pay the government a $129 million settlement. The disaster prompted Congress, in 1980, to enact the Superfund law, which established a cleanup program for U.S. toxic waste sites that requires to this day that waste dumpers pay cleanup costs.

- In 1984 the world's worst industrial accident of all time occurred near Bhopal, India. Toxic methyl isocyanate gas—a pesticide ingredient—leaked from a U.S.-owned chemical plant in India, contaminating water and soil in about a one-mile radius. Eventually more than 2,000 human deaths were officially attributed to the hazardous material accident. An estimated 600,000 people filed compensation claims with the Indian government. Union Carbide, the plant's owner, paid $470 million as part of an out-of-court settlement in 1989. The accident is still a political hot potato in India.

• In 1989 on its way from the Trans Alaska Pipeline, the 986-foot supertanker Exxon Valdez ran aground on a reef off the coast of Alaska and spilled some 11 million gallons of oil. About 1,300 miles of shoreline were affected by the spill, which took more than 10,000 workers four years to battle before they gave up. Hundreds of thousands of birds, sea otters, harbor seals, bald eagles, and whales and billions of fish and fish eggs were killed. Exxon estimated the cleanup effort cost $2.1 billion.

Of course, the United States does not have a patent on toxic-release accidents or oil spills. For instance, a Japanese chemical company CEO dealt with the catastrophic airborne dioxin release that caused human illnesses and the deaths of 100,000 animals in Seveso in the late 1970s.

While the vast majority of the other toxic threats, incidents, and aftermaths discussed in this book are more pedestrian than those mentioned above, they are nonetheless matters taken seriously by CEOs and other toxic corporate leaders who have had to deal with them.

Therefore, the focus of this book is how U.S. companies and their personnel can become proactive nontoxic leaders. It's all designed to help ensure that catastrophes—large or small—don't occur in the future.

The disaster that was 9/11 created a great deal of controversy, soul-searching, and preparation in the chemical manufacturing and usage arenas—as it should. In the afterword to this section, I will deal directly with how you can better protect yourself from a once rarely considered threat: a terrorist attack that could cause a hazardous chemical release. But, for now, let's look at some everyday toxic challenges chemicals pose for you, your company, and your employees.

HOW SAFE ARE OUR WORKERS?

Every corporate leader whose company deals with hazardous chemicals must acknowledge that employees' lives are riding on the safety of your daily operations. It's a sobering thought. EHS professionals certainly understand this challenge; it's what they think about every day.

When you work with hazardous chemicals, you never know when a life-threatening situation will arise. I can personally attest to this as I had a couple of near misses during my summer-job days while in college.

In 1967 I worked summers as a cleanup person in the local mill in Camas, Washington. On two occasions my life was unknowingly put at risk while working with chemicals. In the first, I was temporarily trapped in a 1910-vintage boiler exhaust flue, when partially combusted organics caught fire during a routine downtime cleaning. On another occasion, I was accidentally drenched in a caustic solution by an overzealous coworker during a large tank clean-out session. In both cases I was lucky. Quick action by my coworkers and me literally saved my life.

Had things gone differently in my two near-miss encounters with hazardous chemicals, my life could have ended and my story would have been shortened considerably. My four daughters never would have been born. My company would not have been formed, and the list goes on. And each of us, each of our workers, has a rich future to protect.

In 1967 it was not having an excellent hazardous chemical information database available and extensive formal safety training that kept us safe; it was our common sense. Today companies pride themselves on implementing more sophisticated and systematic training procedures. But have businesses done enough? My current company, Dolphin Software, helps companies with their chemical management challenges. In the course of that work, our employees have twice, through the expedient transmission of vital hazard communication information to medical workers, been able to help save the lives of clients' workers who were involved in chemical mishaps. How many near-miss stories can you and your EHS people remember?

We've probably all complained about how nice it would be if we didn't have OSHA forms to fill out and OSHA inspections to worry about. But then again, when people's lives are at stake, safety must come first. Wasting our most valuable resource, *our people*, would be the biggest mistake of all!

Training and equipping our people to be safer when handling chemicals is a vital component of a solid chemical management program. And safety is definitely one of the goals—the protecting-your-people piece—of a CSTCM program.

The so-called "general duty clause" that dictates OSHA's safety policy couldn't be more clear: "Each Employer shall furnish to each of his employees, employment and a place of employment which are free from recognized hazards that are causing or likely to cause death or serious physical harm to its employees." If your company must, in its daily operations, expose workers to hazardous chemicals, you are certainly not alone. OSHA estimates that more than 32 million workers are exposed to 650,000 hazardous chemicals in more than three million workplaces annually. And 500 to 1,000 new chemicals are introduced into the marketplace each year, many of which pose health hazards.

How safe are our workers from all these hazardous chemicals? In the last year for which we have full statistics, worker exposures to hazardous materials accounted for the lowest mortality rate of the major risk categories (including such risks as contact with equipment, falls, fires, and explosions) tracked by the Bureau of Labor Statistics (BLS), which supplies the most complete counting of fatal work injuries.

The BLS categorizes hazardous material-related deaths as "exposure to caustic, noxious, or allergenic substances" or "inhalation of a substance." In 1999, 163 deaths were so recorded. In 2000 there were 148 such deaths. In 2001, the latest year for which figures were available when this book went to press, there were 96 deaths of this nature reported, amounting to only 1.6 percent of the total 5,900 U.S. workplace fatalities for that year. (This does not include any of the 9/11-related deaths.)

Though the statistics are going down, our goal must be *zero* fatalities due to exposure to hazardous materials. How could we have helped prevent those 96 deaths in 2001? And how will *you* help prevent fatalities in the future?

One of the purposes of this book is to convey helpful advice designed to bring hazardous-material workplace death rates down to zero.

HOW HEALTHY IS OUR ENVIRONMENT?

You don't have to be too shrewd an observer to recognize that the news originating from environmental groups is often pessimistic. The truth of the matter is, all the government environmental regulation we have initiated in the United States for the past three or four decades—and the corresponding commitment of the business community to clean up its act—has made an enormous difference for the better.

According to the EPA, since 1988 in the United States there has been a 48 percent decline in toxic releases of the baseline chemicals first measured in the original agency inventory, a reduction of more than 1.53 billion pounds of toxic material a year. The chemical industry itself has reduced toxic releases more than any other industry (see pp. 28-29 for figures on DuPont's savings-producing efforts), with a 76 percent reduction in releases since 1988. All of this pollution reduction has occurred at the same time that the industrial output for the TRI-covered industries increased some 40 percent.

Productivity gains and technological improvements employed by industry in controlling the creation and release of hazardous substances are large contributors to some heartening environmental statistics (extrapolated from the *Index of Leading Environmental Indicators 2002*, released by the Pacific Research Institute, and *Earth Report 2000*, by the Competitive Enterprise Institute, which the *Wall Street Journal* calls "the best environmental think tank in the country"). For example:

- U.S. Water Quality—Water-quality violations of EPA standards in the United States have dropped since the government put limits on the phosphate content of detergents some 35 years ago. Likewise, reductions in phosphorus fertilizer use and point source controls at sewage treatment, food processing, and other industrial plants have helped lower phosphorus levels in our water systems.

- U.S. Air Quality—In recent decades, air pollution trends in the United States have improved dramatically for aggregate emissions of the six "criteria" pollutants under the Clean Air Act. Since the EPA was founded in 1970, these pollutants have declined 29 percent. At the same time the U.S. economy grew 150 percent and auto travel increased by 143 percent. This improvement of the air we breathe is largely due to industrial pollution reduction and prevention measures.

- Worldwide Air Quality—Per-capita CO_2 emissions have remained mostly constant since 1979, though fossil fuel consumption continues to increase. Chlorofluorocarbons (CFCs), which have been shown to be damaging the ozone layer since their introduction in the 1930s, have been banned. The United States alone has spent an estimated $100 billion in phasing out this offending hazardous substance.

Meanwhile, life expectancy increased about 10 percent in the United States between 1970 and 2001. And most cancer rates in the United States have also been declining since 1990, reversing a 20-year trend of increases, according to the American Cancer Society. Part of the lowering of death and cancer rates is directly attributable to technological advances in medicine. But surely the more healthful state of our environment in the past few decades has also contributed.

GOVERNMENT COMPLIANCE IS EXPENSIVE

One of the EPA's most visible programs focused on hazardous chemicals is the TRI. Through that program, corporate managers are required to report the amounts of more than 300 hazardous chemicals transported or released to the air, water, or land on an annual basis by the Emergency Planning and Community Right-to-Know Act ("Right-to-Know") of 1986. The EPA compiles and publishes this Community Right-to-Know data in the annual TRI, which is made fully public.

At the end of this book, you will find a handy timeline of U.S. Government Regulations to bring you up to date on the federal officials who peer with a bright flashlight at everything your company does with hazardous chemicals.

What all this means for you as the overseer of your company's fortunes is something that you probably already know too well: environmental compliance costs plenty. The Pacific Research Institute, in its *Index of Leading Environmental Indicators 2002*, states, "One of the ironies of environmental policies is that we are often told that natural resources are scarce or finite, yet we promulgate regulations as though money was infinite." The report also states that "private sector spending on the environment now reaches into the hundreds of billions of dollars."

For 2001 U.S. EPA enforcement and compliance assurance efforts included a record-setting $4.3 billion in penalties for violators of pollution controls and environmental cleanup. These programs also secured commitments for an estimated reduction of more than 660 million pounds of harmful pollutants and the treatment and safe management of an estimated record 1.84 billion pounds of pollutants. The EPA settled more than 220 civil judicial cases and issued more than 3,200 administrative orders and field citations.

Another sobering statistic is that the EPA's vigorous criminal program resulted in prison sentences totaling 256 years, which is an increase of more than 100 years of jail time over 2000. Finally, criminal violations also carried nearly $95 million in fines and restitution. That translated to a lot of hard knocks for some toxic CEOs and their employees!

In writing *The Nontoxic CEO*, I asked myself a simple question, "If environmental compliance is mandatory and it is never going away, how can companies learn to reap not just people and planet benefits from compliance but profit gains as well?" The good news is that there is a clear way. *Through the proper implementation of CSTCM you may now start seeing compliance not as a burden but as an opportunity.*

GOVERNMENT COMPLIANCE WILL NEVER GO AWAY

For the first 20 years of the EPA's existence, efforts to control industrial pollution were focused on the treatment and disposal of pollutants after they were created. This is the so-called "end-of-pipe" pollution control technique; however, with the advent of the Pollution Prevention Act (PPA) of 1990, the U.S. government first established pollution prevention (P2) as a national goal. Since that time, the EPA's mind-set has focused on P2, which seeks to control pollution at the source and avoid the creation of pollutants in the first place. Lest you think that the federal and state regulators will slacken their demands for pollution control and prevention, you should know that, at the request of several members of Congress, the Government Accounting Office (GAO) completed a February 2001 study that yielded a document tellingly titled "EPA Should Strengthen Its Efforts to Measure and Encourage Pollution Prevention."

The GAO concluded that a dozen years since the PPA was created, we haven't come far enough in P2. It's no longer enough to merely measure and keep your pollution within accepted limits; the government will increasingly push for more proactive pollution prevention.

REGULATION-DRIVEN PREVENTION PAYS

Using the EPA's TRI data, the GAO report states that between 1991 and 1998, approximately one-quarter to one-third of reporting firms implemented at least one pollution prevention measure. The GAO listed the reasons for companies implementing P2 as: 1) the opportunity for a financial return, and 2) the prospect that P2 could improve a company's public or community image. In other words, the reasons most companies implement P2 is first to aid the bottom line, and second to aid their public relations efforts.

Under P2 programs, companies strive to reduce their creation of toxic waste through a variety of methods. The good news is that part of the CSTCM advice you will find in this book is just solid P2 source reduction. It's all about reducing the volume of hazardous chemicals before they enter the waste stream. CSTCM, from a P2 perspective, means:

- Reducing the number of hazardous chemicals purchased/stored/used/disposed of
- Reducing the total amount of hazardous chemicals purchased/used/disposed of
- Substituting more benign chemicals for toxic ones

CSTCM is propagated on the notion that if you do it right, you'll see significant enhancements to your bottom line and you'll be able to generate some good PR for your efforts. This book will walk you through both goals. And you should know that 23 percent of the types of P2 reported by the GAO included TCM-style programs that dealt with raw material reductions and inventory control.

P2 SAVINGS CAN EXCEED YOUR HURDLE RATE

At Dow Chemical Company, an official told the GAO that to justify undertaking any proposed P2 project, the project's rate of return generally has to exceed the "hurdle rate"—a rate of return as great as the return expected of any alternative investment. This is a common story at many corporations, probably yours included. (In the next several chapters I'll talk more about how other companies have exceeded their hurdle rate with CSTCM and how you can, too.)

Dow officials told the GAO that the company's environmental waste plan included a database containing several thousand potential waste-reduction projects. Generally, 80 percent of their emissions are from 20 percent of the sources. Dow ranks each project by cost and waste reduction potential. The objective is to achieve 80 percent of the benefit for 20 percent of the total projected cost. Projects falling below this cutoff are generally not implemented. Dow has been one of the more successful chemical manufacturing companies in the implementation of P2. For instance, Dow launched its Waste Reduction Always Pays (WRAP) program in 1986. In the first ten years of the program at only one plant among Dow's many facilities worldwide, wastes sent to the incinerator were reduced 88 percent and there was a 98 percent improvement in yield. The cost savings were more than $600,000 a year in raw material and incineration costs.

In a report by the DuPont Chemical Company to the World Business Council for Sustainable Development, DuPont's stated ten-year goals for improving its EHS performance worldwide "should yield a 30 to 40 percent return on investment by 2005." This includes $1.3 billion in reducing waste, $96 million in reducing process safety incidents, $50 million in reducing injury and illness incidents, and $34 million in avoiding costs incurred by business interruption, property damage or spill cleanup. DuPont's example is a good one for your company, though you may not reap as much as the estimated $1.8 billion savings on P2 that the chemical manufacturer does. Obviously, the company's P2 chemical management efforts are exceeding DuPont's aggressive hurdle rates. In spite (or because) of all its expensive pollution prevention—estimated by its CEO to cost $550 million in 2000 alone—DuPont is financially robust. The company's total profit was $1.25 billion in 2002.

There are numerous similar examples of innovative nonchemical companies turning P2 into profits. One of the most famous success stories in the annals of U.S. corporate responsibility vis-à-vis EHS is the 3M Company.

The 3M Corporation, which celebrated its 100th birthday in 2002, started the country's first real, widespread environmental program in 1975. That was before the government implemented the Clean Air Act, the Resource Conservation and Recovery Act (RCRA), The Toxic Substances Control Act (TSCA), the Superfund Program, and the Pollution Prevention Act (PPA). Now that's what you call proactive. Between 1990 and 2001, 3M cut volatile organic air emissions by 91 percent, reduced manufacturing releases to water by 84 percent, reduced solid waste by 12 percent (and waste generation rate by 35 percent), and reduced its U.S. EPA TRI by 88 percent.

Clearly, 3M is a company filled with people who are not content with "chopping wood." The work that 3M has done may not fit into the immediate results category Einstein talked about. These kinds of results cost time, people-hours, start-up money, and commitment; however, 3M reaped tangible benefits from these programs. In the 28 years since 3M unveiled its innovative 3P Program (Pollution Prevention Pays), the savings for the company have been substantial—about $900 million. Almost a billion-dollar savings for doing the right thing is icing on the cake.

As these leading companies have shown, there are numerous avenues, using CSTCM, that virtually any company involved with hazardous chemicals can incorporate to reduce product count, volume,

---

FIGURE 2.

Pollution prevention business rewards (according to the World Business Council):

- Improved financial performance
- Reduced costs
- Dramatically improved productivity (with direct savings to the bottom line)
- Improved organizational effectiveness
- Competitive advantage
- Product differentiation and possible price premiums
- New market opportunities
- Reduced potential liabilities
- Decreased risk of adverse publicity
- Better relations with stakeholders
- Increased attractiveness to investors

---

and waste generation. In chapter 1 (*Why You Need CSTCM*), I will show you more ways to better protect your people, planet, and profits. In chapter 2 (*Building the Business Case*), I will give you advice on meeting the hurdle rate at your company.

Additionally, a small but growing segment of the financial community is starting to take notice of companies that have the foresight to do voluntary P2. In 1996 the World Business Council, a coalition of some 120 international companies from twenty major industrial sectors, released its first report on the issue of environmental performance and shareholder value. The Council concluded that environmental drivers can produce myriad benefits (see Figure 2). These are the same kinds of benefits you will see illustrated for CSTCM throughout this book.

RECENT SUCCESS STORIES: SUPPLY-SIDE TCM

For several years now one fairly well-established avenue for American industries to realize savings through better chemical management has come through the supply chain side of business. Helping lead supply-side chemical management solutions is the nonprofit Chemical

Strategies Partnership (CSP), established by the Pew Charitable Trust in 1996, with support from the Heinz Endowments. CSP states on its website that it "seeks to reduce chemical use, waste, risks, and costs through the transformation of the chemical supply chain by redefining the way chemicals are used and sold." This basically means that CSP assists companies (primarily manufacturers) to work in tandem with chemical suppliers, changing the chemical salesperson's role from attempting to increase volume sales to that of a true service provider, who helps the manufacturer actually *reduce* chemical use and costs. CSP, which features a collection of impressive case studies on its website, many of them from the auto industry, hosts periodic workshops and promotes a how-to manual and a cost-analysis tool.

Further evidence that TCM is a growing wave is illustrated in a recent book by two Illinois State University professors, Thomas Bierma and Francis Waterstraat Jr. Their book, *Chemical Management: Reducing Waste and Cost Through Innovative Supply Strategies* (John Wiley & Sons, 2000) is similar to the CSP's activities in that it is supply-chain focused.

Bierma and Waterstraat call their version of this solution "Shared Savings Chemical Management." In their well-researched book, they advise that since old-paradigm supply relationships with manufacturers are wasteful, more sensible systems have suppliers working proactively on P2 strategies and sharing in the profits of clients who are bold (and smart) enough to find a better way. The book, which focuses on five case studies from the automotive industry, also contains the blueprint for a supply-side Shared Savings model that is well worth the more-than $100 book price if you want to learn more about supply-side solutions.

NONTOXIC TIP

CSTCM, AS YOU WILL SEE IN THE FOLLOWING CHAPTERS, IS FRIENDLY TO SMALL-, MID-, AND EVEN LARGE-SIZED COMPANIES USING LOWER VOLUMES OF CHEMICAL PRODUCTS.

THE NEXT WAVE: COMPLIANCE-SIDE TOTAL CHEMICAL MANAGEMENT

I applaud the work of the CSP, the Illinois State professors, and chemical companies that are becoming true service providers. They are seeking to help trigger a fundamental change in the way chemical suppliers service their customers. In some notable cases these programs include a gain-sharing compensation vehicle. It's a sound approach if you want to manage chemicals from the supply side.

That said, supply-side chemical management is primarily better suited to large-volume chemical users. The supply side approach can produce financial benefits for companies like General Motors, or Delta Air Lines, to cite two companies that have used supply-side TCM. But it's a solution less suited for companies that use thousands of chemicals in smaller volumes.

> **NONTOXIC TIP**
>
> CSTCM WORKS, REGARDLESS OF THE BUSINESS SIZE, CHEMICAL USE VOLUME, OR NUMBER OF CHEMICAL VENDORS USED.

Since CSTCM comes at chemical reduction and the attendant cost savings inherent in better chemical management from the regulatory side, it doesn't matter how many chemical products are needed, what their total volume is, or even how many vendors exist to supply those chemicals. A company like GM may be able to focus on a handful of vendors, or even one or two, for products such as paint. But most companies, such as those with dozens or hundreds of far-flung locations, may rely upon thousands of vendors. The task then takes on a much different tone.

In one CSTCM success story I will illustrate how one of our chemical management clients (a giant wood products company) was able to effect a whopping percentage reduction in chemical volumes. This reduction occurred even though the company was using tens of thousands of active chemical products from more than a thousand chemical manufacturers!

The CSTCM paradigm works as well for smaller companies with far fewer chemical products for another reason. Generally, small and

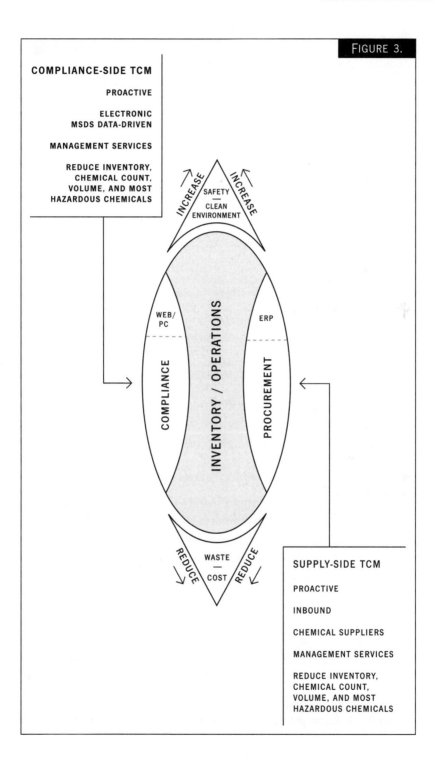

FIGURE 4.

The benefits of CSTCM for your company are many, including:

- Documented chemical history
- Reduced chemical count
- Reduced overbuying
- Reduced total amount of chemicals used
- Elimination of some hazardous chemicals altogether
- Increased worker health and safety
- Consolidated chemicals and suppliers
- Reduced management costs
- Reduced wastes
- Reduced financial exposure to risk
- Increased goodwill among all stakeholders
- Good PR

---

mid-sized companies are shut out of making much progress in implementing P2 measures because they lack the massive technical and financial resources of large companies. CSTCM redresses this lack. The reason is simple. Every company, regardless of size, that is regulated from an EHS standpoint is required to have at its disposal chemical-information-rich Material Safety Data Sheets (MSDSs). Somebody in that company (maybe more than one person) is responsible for worker safety and perhaps has environmental responsibilities also. That means somebody is already keeping track of the pesky MSDSs. And it is through the MSDSs and how their data is handled that CSTCM can provide a company with a clear view of how all chemicals are procured and then highlight significant financial opportunities.

In the coming chapters, you will see that CSTCM is a complete-system approach to chemical management, focusing on true life-cycle costs. We will deal with chemical procurement from a material requests and approvals standpoint—keeping hazards off-site is the first line of action. We will also look at chemical use, handling, monitoring, disposal, and—of course—reporting.

As with any good, money-saving new way of doing business, CSTCM requires a real champion in your organization. If you are the CEO, there is no better champion. Or you may be an executive in charge of EHS, a plant safety manager, or even the night-shift safety worker who is in charge of MSDSs. It scarcely matters. In fact, a lot of people will get involved in your CSTCM success story. It is a truly integrated business model.

By leveraging MSDSs on the compliance side with CSTCM, your company will be able to reap an amazing number of benefits (see Figure 4).

NONTOXIC LEADERSHIP: WHAT YOU MUST DO TO GET IT

Before you read this introduction, if someone had asked, "Why does your company need better chemical management?" your answer might have been something like, "I already know the reasons why better chemical management is a good idea. I just don't have the resources or time to take on a new project or to divert attention from other more critical programs!" We all know that every innovative business program has to stand on its own against all other funding requests. Your job is to prove that implementing a CSTCM program will make money at a higher rate than competing projects. For some of you, recovering your total cost of compliance may be incentive enough!

If you have the courage to stick with this incredibly rewarding chemical management tool waiting within your company's existing compliance machinery, your results will be greater than you ever could have expected.

NONTOXIC TIP

ONE WAY TO GET BUY-IN TO ESTABLISH CSTCM AS A SOUND USE OF COMPANY FUNDS IS BY USING LIFE-CYCLE COSTING (LCC) TECHNIQUES, WHICH WILL BE DISCUSSED LATER IN THIS BOOK.

Now you have gleaned some understanding of why TCM is an idea whose time has come. I'm going to show you in the next chapter why you can't afford not to be doing CSTCM. The best way to illustrate the value of this powerful management system is with real-world examples—case studies and profiles of companies that need or needed CSTCM very badly. One of these stories opens our next chapter and others follow. These real-life examples should help further convince you that you really do need CSTCM.

CHAPTER 1

WHY YOU NEED CSTCM

Here is a true corporate horror story about a major United States company that had an employee who innocently disposed of one partially filled barrel of a highly hazardous chemical. I don't know if it was a dark and stormy night when it happened, as it often is in horror stories, but boy, a storm did rage shortly thereafter!

The company in question got fined millions of dollars for poorly managing this single partial container of chemicals. Then the company got religion and ended up saving millions more dollars through CSTCM.

A CREEPY CASE STUDY, OR HOW TO GO FROM ALARMING TO AWARD-WINNING

It is a seemingly normal night—a number of years ago—at manufacturing company XYZ Widgets (not its real name). XYZ is a global leader in its industry. The corporation has over 100 locations worldwide, employing 60,000 people, more than 250 of whom are EHS specialists. On this particular night, an employee at one of the XYZ facilities pops open one partially filled 55-gallon barrel of "something" that has been sitting around forever. He can't tell what this ancient substance is. It isn't labeled with a skull-and-crossbones. It doesn't smell any worse than the stuff used to clean the kitchen at home. So he figures he'll be tidy and get rid of the old, unusable solution. He dumps it in the nearby drainage ditch that runs to the creek that empties into the river. Hey, it's only a few gallons of liquid dumped into a ditch. How bad could it be?

As with most horror stories, it turned out to be pretty bad. The barrel contained a liquid known as 1,1,1-Trichloro-ethane. This substance was one the first chlorinated organic insecticides, and an infamous one at that. Its use is banned in the United States. Who knows how long it had been sitting in storage, undetected? 1,1,1-Trichloro-ethane is classified as a persistent contaminant in the environment. Instead of being metabolized rapidly by animals, this chemical is deposited and stored in fatty tissues. Its biological half-life is about eight years (meaning it takes an animal about eight years to metabolize half of the amount it assimilates). It's nasty.

Can you guess the next scene in our company's horror story? Enter... not Count Dracula... but someone with equally long fangs: Uncle Sam. After the resultant enforcement citations, XYZ pays a whopping $3 million fine. Three million bucks for the improper disposal of one partly filled 55-gallon drum of a chemical, the contents of which one errant employee at one facility was unaware.

It really happened.

The beginning of our happy ending to this tale is that the incident, that $3 million wake-up call, and motivational leadership inspired the company to manage its chemicals more responsibly. My company suggested the relatively expedient and nonintrusive implementation of CSTCM. *(Note: I want to be clear that you do not have to have a catastrophe to implement CSTCM. You more happily can—and should—do it proactively, no matter your company size, how many chemicals you use, or how clean your safety and environmental records.)*

The upshot for the company was stupendous. By adopting a corporate-wide chemical management standard, XYZ Widgets was able to capture the following benefits:

- Removal of obsolete and out-of-date products from inventory
- Elimination of aerosols
- Avoided stockpiling partially used containers
- Began purchasing smaller quantities of chemicals
- Its formerly poor 8 percent product-overlap between locations later became a cost-effective 60 percent
- Achieved a healthy 70 percent reduction in chemical inventories
- Using compliance dollars and interdepartmental management techniques, they achieved results that were similar to larger manufacturing supply chain programs
- Since implementation they have saved, and are saving millions

TAKING ADVANTAGE OF HIGH-LEVERAGE OPPORTUNITIES

As indicated in the Introduction, Supply-Side Total Chemical Management (SSTCM) has been practiced successfully in the United States for about a decade. SSTCM normally deals with single-vendor chemical accounts in excess of $2 million and entails companies partnering with their chemical suppliers.

To take an example of a company that has undergone SSTCM look at General Motors.

GM has about a dozen plants in North America and a relative handful of vendors for each hazardous substance such as paint lacquer. With GM's sophisticated Enterprise Resource Planning (ERP) system and huge financial clout, SSTCM can be very successful at reducing shelved toxic inventory. GM plants buy a large enough volume and have tight enough control on the number of their vendors, so that they can apply pressure on their suppliers to get better prices.

NONTOXIC TIP

FOR SMALL COMPANIES OR SMALL VOLUME USERS WHO CAN'T PUT PRESSURE ON SUPPLIERS BECAUSE THEY DON'T USE LARGE CHEMICAL VOLUMES, AND FOR LARGE COMPANIES WITH A VAST NUMBER CHEMICAL VENDORS AT SCORES OR HUNDREDS OF LOCATIONS, IT IS BEST TO ADDRESS TOTAL CHEMICAL MANAGEMENT FROM THE COMPLIANCE SIDE.

Supply-side solutions often do not work for high-count, low-volume users because:

1. *Chemicals may be a small part of overall procurement costs.* (Note: In some ways this fact lends itself to being managed by the compliance team whose focus is primarily chemical approval and risk management.)

   • Management support of TCM programs is hard to secure and maintain

   • Periodic financial reporting becomes imperative

2. *Regional, low-volume, or single-chemical product suppliers may not be capable of responding to SSTCM requirements.*

   • Internal resources may be required to augment their limitations

3. *Chemical management departments may not be able to keep the focus on execution over a long period of time.*

   • Requires development of legacy protocols and Standard Operating Procedures (SOPs)

CSTCM HAS WIDER APPLICATIONS

CSTCM begins with automation of the compliance motion that is already in place in most companies. The system will be most effective where chemical procurement utilizes many vendors and smaller volumes. CSTCM has many advantages over large, ERP system/ supply-side solutions in these applications. CSTCM deals with the value of all chemicals in the aggregate.

In the case of XYZ Widgets, SSTCM was wrong for the company, but CSTCM was just right for them because of the very large number of chemicals and vendors over its enterprise system. Many of those vendors deal in small volumes. In fact, the company used more than 40,000 active products, represented by 6,000 manufacturers. Obviously, not every one of our sample company's 40,000-plus chemicals are hazardous. But even though not every chemical required reporting, each was regulated. That means OSHA required the company to have an MSDS for each of the more than 40,000 unique chemicals. (That's essential to CSTCM!).

How companies could take advantage of both SSTCM and CSTCM simultaneously might be the subject of a future book. For now, however, I would like to focus on compliance-side solutions. A valuable CSTCM program can, of course, be run solo with plenty of financial, environmental, and safety returns.

NONTOXIC TIP

FOR THE RIGHT COMPANIES, CHEMICAL MANAGEMENT PROGRAMS SHOULD INCORPORATE *BOTH* SSTCM AND CSTCM.

REDUCING HAZARDOUS CHEMICALS IS KEY

Using CSTCM, our goal at XYZ Widgets was to reduce its inventory, and subsequently its waste and financial exposure.

Think of it! Less working capital tied to inventory, less material to handle and store, fewer waste products to transport and fewer dollars spent on disposal. You'll have less corporate-wide exposure to potential spills, injuries, or accidents. And for some of you with better information on local purchasing practices, you'll have more efficient procurement, too!

NONTOXIC TIP

IF WE CAN CUT THE NUMBER AND VOLUME OF CHEMICALS IN USE IN OUR BUSINESSES, WE WILL REDUCE OPERATIONAL COSTS.

CASE STUDY OF AN IMPLEMENTATION: "TOXIC" UTILITY

Shortly before this book went to press, my company was asked to travel to and consult with a $10 billion utility with more than 60 locations, including its group of nearly a dozen giant power-generation facilities. I'll call the client Power-Co, Inc. (PCI).

Initially, PCI asked us to consult with them on the ongoing automation of the vast database of MSDSs that they are required to keep on the more than 10,000 chemical products used in their daily operations. The company had been saving some $300,000 a year by automating MSDSs, as opposed to dealing with them in hard copy. But the executives had not attempted to do any TCM from the compliance side using their MSDSs and their rich vein of related chemical information.

We used PCI's automated MSDS data (constituting more than 111,000 pages of chemical information) as the basis of a possible CSTCM solution. What my company found out about our utility client shocked us, and really shocked PCI personnel—including their EHS people, financial folks, and executives.

The careful MSDS examinations revealed that:

- Of the 10,000-plus products the company uses, only 11 percent are used at more than one of the corporate locations
- Nearly 8,000 of the products were single-site exclusives!

In short, what PCI had on its hands was an inefficient, grossly expensive, chemical management nightmare. My company drilled down a little deeper into the MSDS chemical-data gold mine and came up with some startling environmental-ingredient analysis. PCI had an unmanaged, multivendor mess on its hands. Working with the utility, we immediately targeted the following obvious products for reduction through better procurement:

- Acetone (10 different vendors for this common product)
- PCP Treated Wood (more than 15 vendors)
- Hydrochloric Acid (more than 10 vendors)
- Sulfuric Acid (more than 10 vendors)
- Adhesives (more than 200 varieties)
- Solvents (more than 100 varieties)
- Paints (more than 150 varieties)
- Oils (more than 400 varieties)

As we went through the data, we could see the PCI executives and EHS people turning pale. How many vendors do you need for acetone? One? Two? OK, maybe even three. But 10? How many types of adhesives do you need to run through your purchasing department? Of course, the answer is a lot fewer than 200. And oil? Maybe PCI needs 100 different oils, but they don't need well over 400 different varieties! Until we applied an initial CSTCM inspection to its inventories, the company had no idea of what they had, or how much of it, or what was obsolete, unneeded, or out of date.

And that was good news in comparison to other revelations.

It got worse when we asked the automated MSDS data to "give me your poor, your downtrodden, your carcinogenic, and mutagenic." Here are just some of the deadly toxins—notorious carcinogens, groundwater pollutants, and hazardous substances—that we easily found that same day by applying CSTCM:

- More than 100 products that contained lead or lead compounds
- Almost 50 products that contained trichloro-ethylene (TCE)
- More than 70 products that contained perchloroethylene (PCE)
- More than 50 products that contained mercury or mercury compounds

FIGURE 5.

Estimated Utility Company Chemical Inventory Annual Savings
Based on 2002 chemical transactions.

1. Central Stores Purchases: $6 million
   - 60 sites
   - 1,000 SKUs
   - ~33 percent of MSDS inventory

2. Purchase ("P") Card Purchases: $10 million
   - Based on figures above

3. Estimated Inventory Reduction/Working Capital Improvement
   - 20 percent = $4 million
   - 30 percent = $6 million
   - 40 percent = $8 million
   - 50 percent = $10 million

The moment of revelation came when we applied the numbers to what PCI would save as it implemented painless CSTCM chemical reductions (see Figure 5).

If PCI completes a 50 percent reduction of its chemical nightmare (remember that in the XYZ Widgets case study in chapter 1, that company accomplished a 70 percent reduction of chemical inventories) the East Coast utility will start to achieve a $10 million inventory reduction. Even if PCI only accomplishes a modest 30 percent reduction of chemicals, they stand to cut $6 million out of inventory. That's real economic recovery through CSTCM. And it doesn't begin to address the many benefits in worker safety, greater environmental health, better PR, and greatly reduced corporate liabilities.

Are you seeing even more clearly the need to become a nontoxic CEO?

Before you cluck your tongue too loudly about the utility's chemical management practices (or lack thereof), don't be so sure that your company would fare much better—if you haven't applied CSTCM.

Our extensive work with some leading companies shows very little optimization on product use and application across operations.

POLLUTION PREVENTION IS ALSO KEY

Part of the CSTCM advice you will find in this book, which uses MSDSs as a starting point, is just solid, old-fashioned, pollution prevention, or P2 source reduction. It's all about reducing the amount of hazardous substances before they enter the workplace. And there are a lot of ways you can do that from the compliance side.

The benefits of P2 through robust CSTCM are obvious. The kinds of things we asked XYZ Widgets and told them they should do through CSTCM are similar to those things you will hear from your CSTCM team and/or consultants. These suggestions are:

- Given your exposure over multiple sites, get rid of a specific A-list of products first (those that are most toxic or pose other threats). Get rid of a B-list of products second. Lose the C-list products third. Put a formal materials request and approval process in place prior to procurement so that none of these products make it back into your facilities.

- Look at product count at each site over the course of time.

- Reduce the vendor count and the number of different products you buy, limiting the product characteristics that are coming into each site. Reducing vendor count means buying from fewer vendors.

- Evaluate needs and what is appropriate at each location. Consider using a blanket chemical provider (consolidator).

- Work to prevent overbuying and under-buying.

- Look at product obsolescence. Do you have products on your shelves that are becoming something hazardous just because of age? Do you have products you didn't use or get rid of when you should have?

- Look at inventory levels and assigned inventory value (if you bring inventory down, working capital will increase).

- Consider our recommended product substitutions (less hazardous alternative substances).

- Label everything properly.

- Smooth out your reporting to agencies.

- Simplify procurement.
- You're going to like the savings in administrative time, and the economic impacts will cover project costs and contribute to your bottom line.

WE LOOK AT TRUE LIFE-CYCLE COSTS

There have been many studies to show that the actual cost of hazardous chemicals throughout their life cycles is much more than the cost of the products themselves.

> **NONTOXIC TIP**
>
> STUDIES SHOW THE LIFE-CYCLE COST OF A CHEMICAL RANGES FROM TWICE TO TEN TIMES THE ORIGINAL PRODUCT PRICE.

The life cycle of a hazardous chemical forces you into all kinds of other expenditures. You've got to buy the safety equipment to handle the chemical safely and train people to handle it properly. You've got to store it, label it, clean up after it, and fix machines damaged by invasive chemicals. Then you've got to dispose of it and report it to the government. If you don't you may have to pay for toxic chemical-related environmental cleanups, government penalties, sick time, and/or related death benefits, settlements, litigation fees, and other exposure issues.

Using less hazardous chemicals (where possible) and reducing your chemical count and volume overall will substantially lower your costs all around. Working with chemicals may sometimes be science, but managing them better is not rocket science; however, it does take a commitment of time and effort and some initial expenditures. In the case of XYZ Widgets, the company started by building a set of audit questions that each site would be responsible for to indicate what they had done or were doing in chemical management.

In section 2 of this book, which covers auditing and implementation, you will see that your company will have to look at many aspects of how it deals with chemicals. You'll examine the site coordination, written plan, chemical approval process, and tracking processes throughout the system. You'll have to look at your chemical inventories, the amount of compliance that you have to do, and the economic benefits. And it will all be worth the effort.

NONTOXIC TIP

CHEMICALS HAVE LONG AND COSTLY LIFE CYCLES, AND THAT ALONE IS A GOOD REASON FOR CSTCM.

STOP LIVING IN COMPLIANCE FEAR

Beyond the obvious benefits of safety, environmental, and fiscal health, another key reason that you need CSTCM as a nontoxic CEO is that you and your people need to change your focus with regard to compliance. Put simply: you need to stop living in compliance fear. And you need to stop viewing compliance as a lost cost of doing business.

Currently, the vast majority of U.S. businesses are approaching compliance as something they are forced to do by the government, instead of seeing compliance as a way save money. The question most asked by companies living in compliance fear is "How do we make sure we are prepared for that rare but possible OSHA audit?" Your company's senior EHS director may be prompted to ask, "How can we be confident that our engineering-level mathematics will stand up to an EPA review?"

Inventory and ingredient-level data can be so complex that it is almost impossible to be confident that an environmental audit accounts for everything. A recurring nightmare is waking up wondering if you have properly educated your operations personnel to control the use and disposal of workplace chemicals. (XYZ Widgets can tell you a thing or two million about that!)

Stop thinking about your safety and environmental people as staff groups. Start thinking about them as part of your operating processes. Then, instead of seeing them as a dreaded cost of doing business or compliance cost, you will begin to see the work they do as a vital add-on to your operational process. Compliance, when properly done, requires a new way of looking at purchasing and handling inventory, reducing the amount of required compliance reporting, and reducing the amount of necessary personal protective equipment—all of the good things for people, planet, and profits.

Yes, you are going to comply. You are going to meet OSHA and EPA standards. But as a nontoxic CEO, you are going to make compliance part of the integrated operating environment and your more lean-and-effective integrated leadership style. Then you will truly see the significance of your compliance motion in an operating sense and you will realize its powerful value to your bottom line.

NONTOXIC TIP

WHAT IS FUNDAMENTAL TO CSTCM IS FUNDAMENTAL TO MANAGING YOUR CHEMICALS AND YOUR WHOLE OPERATION. START SEEING THE COMPLIANCE STAFF AS CORE TO OPERATIONS, NOT JUST AS PART OF YOUR MANDATORY COMPLIANCE.

LEVERAGE YOUR EXISTING COMPLIANCE EFFORTS

By approaching chemical management from the compliance side you will work comfortably within an existing organizational structure that already works at your company. *CSTCM is a system of better management and a cost-savings-generator that fits neatly into your legacy compliance structure.*

In the case of XYZ Widgets, the company substantially reduced its chemical inventory carrying cost, which was a huge economic driver. Since the company's myriad sites were purchasing from more than 6,500 suppliers it had no idea how much its chemical inventory was costing. The company didn't even know what the inventory was because it had so much local purchasing going on at hundreds of locations.

The only way to get a fix on something that spread out is from the compliance side and the visibility that automated MSDSs will give you. Since each chemical is required to have a corresponding MSDS, chemicals can be carefully tracked and controlled through that compliance doorway. And while it may not be an elegant ERP solution, it sure is effective!

A HAPPY ENDING: SAFER, CLEANER, MORE PROFITABLE

The results of our CSTCM experience with XYZ Widgets couldn't have turned out better. Besides making the company's EHS department a margin manager, the CSTCM program won XYZ's "President's Award." XYZ was also recently voted one of the safest companies in the country by a leading safety organization.

EACH COMPANY'S NEEDS DIFFER

Not all industries are the same, of course. If you're in a Food and Drug Administration (FDA)-regulated industry, you face tougher controls. If you're a pharmaceutical company or if you provide products that people consume, the chances of you having a toxic product impact in a pill or food product is remote. That said, of course, significant CSTCM savings are available to pharmaceutical companies by managing laboratory chemical shelf life and inter-lab availability. If you are in a process or manufacturing environment, the probability of your having toxic products in the workplace is much greater. You will have to be more diligent.

The traditional motives that fuel people to do a good job with TCM are financial. Nontoxic CEOs can feel good about this, as long as they also care about human safety, the environment, and social responsibility.

STAY AHEAD OF THE COMPETITION

You may add a couple more items to your list of reasons for implementing CSTCM. First, you want to stay ahead of the game. If your competition is not already doing CSTCM, they may be planning for it. And second, your customers will increasingly expect you to manage chemicals better.

The overwhelming reason most businesses implement better chemical management is that it saves them money and makes them more competitive. While surfing the Internet for competitor innovations in this arena, you will find that many companies are getting involved in better EHS management in general and smarter chemical management in particular.

FIGURE 6.

Major corporations that have implemented some form of TCM in recent years (by industry):

- **Automotive/Transportation:** Ford, GM, DaimlerChrysler, Harley-Davidson
- **Aviation:** Boeing Company, Delta Air Lines
- **Chemical Manufacturers:** Dow, DuPont, Monsanto
- **Consumer Products:** 3M
- **Defense/Aerospace:** Raytheon
- **Family/Personal Care:** Johnson & Johnson, Proctor & Gamble
- **High-Tech:** HP, IBM, Microsoft, United Technologies
- **Metals:** Alcoa
- **Oil and Gas:** BP, Shell
- **Pharmaceuticals/Health:** Bristol-Meyers Squibb, Merck, Novartis, Pfizer, Pharmacia
- **Pulp and Paper:** International Paper Company, Georgia Pacific, Weyerhaeuser
- **Retail:** Home Depot

Environmental think tanks such as the World Resources Institute promote P2 and greater hazardous materials risk abatement because they lend competitive advantages to businesses. The Global Environmental Management Initiative (GEMI) has more than 40 corporate members who exchange information on how to better manage their EHS operations.

In Figure 6, you will find a box listing just a fraction of the major corporations that are collectively spending billions of dollars on well-publicized EHS efforts. And most of these companies claim there are strong financial rewards for them to do more.

There is no better endorsement for the financial soundness of TCM than this list of advocates. You know that if these companies are doing TCM, it pays.

These companies are not merely complying with government regulations. And lest you say, "It's easy for them to do; they're all corporate giants who can afford it," the truth is, they can't afford not to go beyond compliance in today's marketplace, and neither can you.

Since you are reading this book you are probably the type of person who wants to leave a positive organizational legacy. What better legacy to leave than providing a safer work environment, a cleaner world, and an even more financially robust operation?

You will find that the legacy benefit of CSTCM is one of your most rewarding, so use it as you steel yourself to be the corporate champion who takes part in the initial implementation, ongoing maintenance, and employee/partner motivation that will be required to deliver a truly successful, long-term program.

BE PREPARED FOR SKEPTICISM AND "NAYSAYERS"

At this point you may be convinced that CSTCM will be able to help your company lower toxic waste and chemical costs; at the same time it will increase safety, environmental health, and profits. But you will still have an uphill battle in convincing other stakeholders of the value of managing chemicals better. These stakeholders will include your fellow executives and employees, perhaps vendors and other partners, and maybe even the shareholders.

Of course, complex implementations at any corporation will be culturally challenging and may be viewed by some as organizationally difficult or impossible. Naysayers are nothing new; in fact, on the upside they often add a needed element of perspective and objectivity. Other points of view are healthy. Doing the difficult is only possible for visionary leaders, when you and your organization have taken a universal view and have clearly calculated the long-term risks and benefits of undertaking any paradigm shift.

IDENTIFY A BANDLEADER

A strong champion or bandleader for any sound corporate program requires organizational intelligence and communication skills. The bandleader will not only have to tell everyone why the program you are about to launch is an outstanding idea, but that person will also have to make sure everyone stays fired up about the program. If you are that champion, the scope of full CSTCM will demand that you look not only to technology but also to a highly effective cross-functional team. It is vitally important that you harmonize and integrate your diverse objectives and comprehend how they are affected by your company's unique corporate culture.

But how often does a multifaceted business organization truly work as a harmonious, well-oiled machine? Not nearly as often as we would like! The best illustration of multi-input integration I have witnessed in recent years occurred at Disney World in Orlando, Florida, while I watched a spectacular holiday concert.

On a clear December's evening, a full 80-piece symphony orchestra sat, ringed by a 100-member professional choir, a high-school choir made up of kids from 20 states, and assorted Hollywood celebrities. This gigantic ensemble stood ready, rehearsed, and poised for performance. Each participant awaited the conductor's direction to gift the audience a rare musical interpretation of Handel's *Messiah*.

I was the CEO of a small software company struggling to maintain an aggressive 30 percent-plus growth and profitability. Quite a few employees had been hired over a short period of time. Unfortunately, the diverse, uncoordinated objectives were stifling financial performance. Not surprisingly, company morale was suffering.

Right before the conductor at Disney World raised his baton, I had a moment of enlightenment. What if the soprano section decided that they were bored with the "Hallelujah Chorus" and in the middle of their performance decided to sing Sonny and Cher's "I Got You Babe"? And what if, at that same moment, the high-school choir launched in a song by the Dave Matthews Band, and the Hollywood celebrity narrator read from Edgar Allen Poe's *The Raven*, instead of the Christmas story? What would have been the quality of the experience for the Walt

Disney musical audience? Likely chaos, frustration, anger, and complaints would abound. I would be asking for my money back.

All of this, of course, did not happen. The conductor confidently guided his musicians and singers through to a truly exhilarating, mountain-top experience. But it was only because everyone understood his or her unique contribution to the whole and because an impassioned bandleader conducted everyone in harmony.

When we see so many companies today operating in their own, compartmentalized departmental "silos," with different departmental personnel singing their own tunes, is it surprising to find our organizations incapable of sustaining paradigm-shifting programs such as TCM? Environmental people don't talk to the safety people. Procurement is unaware of the needs for chemical approval. IT has different objectives still. And you, as an unintentional toxic CEO, listen to chaos, trying to decipher a recognizable, financially robust tune.

Don't worry; with strong, inspiring leadership, a good plan, and the financial justifications in place, you'll win all the hearts and minds you need for success. The next steps are answering the money questions and building your business case for CSTCM to sell the program to other people in your organization.

NONTOXIC TIP

AS YOU UNDERTAKE THE ROLE OF CSTCM BANDLEADER YOU WILL BE FACED WITH THE NEED TO COMMUNICATE THE MESSAGE OF THE MUSIC: THE VALUES.

FIGURE 7.

CSTCM benefits, working through the compliance machinery at your company, include:

- Leveraging established compliance budgets
- Can be administered by compliance staff
- Utilizing local EHS expertise
- Utilizing low-cost enterprise (Web) software
- Can be applied in stages
- High rates of return

CHAPTER 2

BUILDING THE BUSINESS CASE

In the literary world, there is disagreement over the origin of the popular phrase "The road to hell is paved with good intentions." Though the remark is often attributed to the tireless British wit Samuel Johnson, some feel an earlier French or English writer may have pronounced it first. Regardless of who coined the expression, it is a phrase that CEOs—toxic and otherwise—have occasion to ponder frequently.

More precisely, the road to failed better-management programs is too frequently paved with our good intentions. But no matter how good your early inspiration for a program, when an idea is dead at your company, it's dead. To implement a truly successful CSTCM program, therefore, you will need a lot more than good intentions.

You are going to need:

- Senior management leadership
- Budget for CSTCM (don't worry, hurdle rate will be met)
- Help from a lot of people in different departments (remember, this is an integrated program)
- At least one stalwart CSTCM champion (someone with real passion)

And before you can have any of the above necessary elements, you will need to be able to build a sound business case for CSTCM. That's what I hope to help you do in this chapter, whether you are trying to get an innovative pilot program off the ground at one facility or attempting a widely beneficial (and challenging) enterprise solution. I will help you sell your program idea(s) by:

- Showing you how to save time and money in administration, management, and compliance reporting through automation of your MSDSs
- Suggesting approaches for chemical reductions and ways to free up working capital through inventory reduction
- Alerting you to chemical-substitution opportunities that can yield multiple benefits, not the least of which will be waste system reductions

- Providing you with financial guidelines for calculating both MSDS-automation and chemical-reduction savings

ESTABLISH YOUR FINANCIAL JUSTIFICATION

In a business setting, the value of any new program will always need to move beyond the soft benefits and directly reflect the expected financial returns.

I recently read an insightful white paper entitled *Overcoming Organizational Snags to Technology Transfer,* by Jonathan Worstell of the Shell Chemical Company. In the piece, Worstell says that in the project he was studying, and in projects in general, "the rate-limiting step (or snag) … was the acquisition of the AFE, the Authorization For Expenditure. It is difficult to shorten the time required for acquiring an AFE, because every corporation has rules for applying for capital. Asking for funds means taking a risk, but that is generally the difference between highly successful organizations and those that are not. The former takes and manages risk while the latter avoids it."

You certainly don't want to limit your potential for capturing all the protection you can through CSTCM. Don't be afraid to seek the money to do the program! That's what this chapter will help you do— take a worthwhile risk.

Instead of delivering to you a canned approach for calculating rate of return, let's look at actual results and case studies that demonstrate the magnitude of CSTCM opportunities. These examples will help you establish enough credibility within your company to launch an investigation of CSTCM's potential.

THE IMPORTANCE OF REDUCING RISK

For many businesses, chemical-risk reduction is a compelling reason to fund chemical management programs. Fear is a great motivator. We are predisposed to prevent loss. Look at the vitality of the pre-9/11 insurance industry. We spend significant insurance dollars each year preparing for the financial impacts of unforeseen and improbable accidents. This mind-set is an important part of quite a number of board-level deliberations.

So where does the primary fear or risk-avoidance incentive reside when it comes to chemical management? Fear of OSHA noncompliance is not a driver, since the penalty structure does not create the kind of economic negatives necessary to change legacy practices. OSHA Hazard Communication (HAZCOM) compliance occurs because a corporation has an established value around protecting its people, or at the very least needs to be viewed as socially responsible.

EPA fines and enforcement actions, on the other hand, are financially compelling. EPA enforcement and compliance-assurance efforts yielded a record-setting $4.3 billion in penalties for violators of pollution controls and environmental cleanup in 2001. The EPA settled more than 220 civil judicial cases and issued more than 3,200 administrative orders and field citations. And the Agency's vigorous criminal program has resulted in prison sentences totaling 256 years and carrying nearly $95 million in fines and restitution. Although much more of an unknown, fear of employee litigation over accidents, injuries, or sickness and years of court battles could also prove a compelling force.

A recently published paper by The Global Environmental Management Initiative (GEMI), *New Paths to Business Value Strategic Sourcing—Environmental, Health and Safety*, speaks to the need to assess EHS risk. In this document, a checklist was developed to assess EHS impacts, risks, and value opportunities. An amazing 76 percent of the categories listed involved the need to better manage chemicals in the workplace.

REACH ABOVE THE LOW-HANGING FRUIT

Where do you start to justify sound chemical management?

Too often the EHS professionals building a sound business case for managing their compliance stop at considering ways to do their existing jobs more efficiently. Most would probably be satisfied with being able to optimize their daily routine. Logically, that leads to automating their MSDSs and other reporting requirements, which normally yields annual returns on investment in a range of 15 to 50 percent. That's pretty good return. But why not reach higher? All the rewarding chemical reduction of CSTCM will be influenced by MSDS data on your chemical inventories.

> ### NONTOXIC TIP
>
> BECAUSE IMPLEMENTING A FINANCIALLY REWARDING CSTCM PROGRAM WILL BEGIN WITH AUTOMATION OF YOUR MSDSs, BUILDING YOUR BUSINESS CASE FOR CSTCM REWARDS MUST BEGIN WITH YOUR EHS COMPLIANCE.

Increasing the Return On Investment (ROI) to hundreds of thousands or even millions of dollar, requires a certain degree of courage and risk-taking. But before we explore acquisition and inventory management, let's review MSDS automation.

ADMINISTRATIVE RECOVERY THROUGH MSDS AUTOMATION

Every third-party MSDS software vendor in the market has put forth his or her particular version of an MSDS ROI calculator. All of these approaches are similar. They all call for an audit of time and cost expenditures associated with manual MSDS management methods. This process is the same whether you automate by putting your chemical data on the Internet, by using software, or with one of the available Application Service Provider (ASP) solutions.

At the end of the mathematical chewing and spreadsheet work, some practitioners point to astronomical returns. The reality is, automation does pay, but at a 15 to 50 percent annual rate of return after the end user's total cost of managing technology is considered. Certainly, this is still a very attractive and a competitive return.

The upper end of the scale in recovery value from MSDS automation is only approachable for operations with multiple locations, or over the breadth of an enterprise. A chemically nonintense operation with a small, single site and less than 150 to 200 MSDSs (most of which are likely maintenance product sheets) may find the investment questionable.

Franchise operations with similar or identical retail stores are exceptions to the above example. Under the right circumstances they also can benefit greatly from low-cost, Web-based MSDS data centralization. In this case a few hundred MSDSs can be published to hundreds or even thousands of sites. Large multinational franchisers need to

---

FIGURE 8.

Typical Administrative Cost Recovery Model for MSDS Automation:

1. Average hourly wage or monthly salary by job classification

2. Overhead loading factor

3. Time spent weekly or monthly in MSDS management
   a. Direct administration for HAZCOM, including updating folders or files
   b. Direct administration for EPA reporting
   c. Direct time preparing maintenance employees for chemically intense jobs

4. Percentage of chemical products introduced as new products each year

5. Percentage of MSDS turnover due to revision activity

6. Enterprise specific data:
   a. MSDS counts for each site by business unit
   b. Percentage of chemical products commonly used

7. EPA and OSHA fines in the last five years

---

smooth relatively low compliance costs over all operations to rationalize automation.

All methods of compliance still require employee notification and training that may be difficult due to end-user technology and leadership communication infrastructure limitations.

FIGURE 9.

Forest Products CSTCM: Chemical Usage

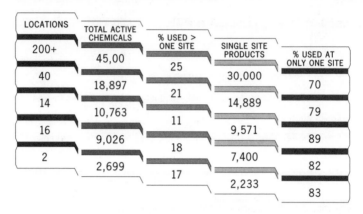

LOCATIONS	TOTAL ACTIVE CHEMICALS	% USED > ONE SITE	SINGLE SITE PRODUCTS	% USED AT ONLY ONE SITE
200+	45,00	25	30,000	70
40	18,897	21	14,889	79
14	10,763	11	9,571	89
16	9,026	18	7,400	82
2	2,699	17	2,233	83

Listed above is chemical use data from five forest products companies of various sizes. All companies utilize local purchasing to fulfill the minor chemical needs of their operations. In all cases more than 70 percent of a company's chemical products are used in just one location. Obviously many different products are being purchased for the same function and from a large set of vendor suppliers. Taken in the aggregate, this chemical use profile costs these companies millions in procurement transaction fees, administrative compliance costs, working capital inventory that carries charges, and waste disposal expense.

Opportunities to reduce chemical product and vendor count will include material standardization between facilities and procurement optimization that focuses on selecting fewer vendors, fewer products, and more volume per product. Most CSTCM programs begin with toxic product reduction and then shift to consolidation of Maintenance, Repair, and Operations (MRO) chemicals.

FIGURE 10.

Pharmaceutical CSTCM: Chemical Usage

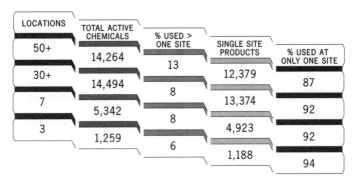

LOCATIONS	TOTAL ACTIVE CHEMICALS	% USED > ONE SITE	SINGLE SITE PRODUCTS	% USED AT ONLY ONE SITE
50+	14,264	13	12,379	87
30+	14,494	8	13,374	92
7	5,342	8	4,923	92
3	1,259	6	1,188	94

Surprisingly the Pharmaceutical Industry has the highest percentage of chemicals purchased for use at a single site! One might think that because of FDA requirements that chemical products might be more closely scrutinized and more chemicals might be commonly used between sites. As we can see, the opposite is true. Why?

Several factors may be contributing:

- Research and Development scientists may insist on particular or rare chemicals or on ordering their own brand of chemicals

- A clean industry is less diligent in managing workplace exposure

- Margins in the business are traditionally high and smaller volume chemical purchases receive less review

Since bench chemicals are supplied by relatively few chemical manufacturers and distributors, the balance of chemicals in this industry should be facility maintenance products. The opportunity for improving chemical use profiles is good.

FIGURE 11.

Power Utilities CSTCM: Chemical Usage

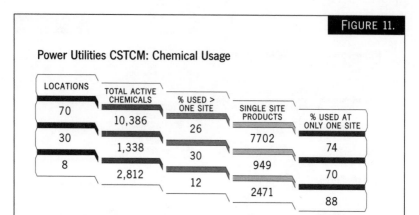

LOCATIONS	TOTAL ACTIVE CHEMICALS	% USED > ONE SITE	SINGLE SITE PRODUCTS	% USED AT ONLY ONE SITE
70	10,386	26	7702	74
30	1,338	30	949	70
8	2,812	12	2471	88

Three power utility companies' chemical product use profiles show that between 70 to 88 percent of chemical products have been purchased as one-off use materials. Since most companies in this sector are regionally focused, there are good opportunities to find common suppliers and commonly useable products through CSTCM.

Note: Uncontrolled indiscriminate local chemical purchases introduces unwanted toxins into the workplace environment.

CALCULATING WHAT MSDS MANAGEMENT COSTS: A CASE STUDY

Here are a couple of guidelines to help you calculate what it should cost to manage the average MSDS.

First, the OSHA-published data on MSDS use is helpful to set up one version of a calculator. This work develops a cost-per-MSDS for a well-managed MSDS hard copy system, using conservative operational assumptions. For instance:

- OSHA has stated that 84 percent of all MSDS are handled twice yearly
- Each handling averages 15 minutes in length
- Assume a loaded labor and overhead charge of $30 per hour
- Assume 100 MSDSs in the database

84 MSDSs handled yearly × 2 times per year × 30 minutes apiece =

2,520 minutes / 60 minutes =

42 hours × $30 per hour =

$1,260 per year labor / 100 MSDS =

$12.60 per MSDS

There are numerous company-specific case studies that have confirmed that $12 to $16 per MSDS is spent to fully manage a hard copy compliance system every year.

A $20 billion, world-leading packaged foods company approached the exercise a bit differently. A calculation was developed based on the average time spent at each location managing MSDSs. This company's data illustrates two points. First, the cost-per-MSDS is in the same range as the OSHA-based approach. Second, it shows a multiple-site advantage. Note that a 25 percent labor-cost advantage can be attained by electronically centralizing MSDS information.

World-Leading Packaged Foods Company Example:
- MSDSs are handled 9.4 hours per month, per site
- There are 103 sites
- There are a total of 36,435 MSDSs
- Assume a 10 percent duplication rate and 25 percent crossover rate between sites
- Total of 24,593 unique MSDSs

$$9.4 \text{ hours per month} \times 103 \text{ sites} =$$

$$968 \text{ hours per month} \times 12 \text{ months} =$$

$$11,616 \text{ hours per year} \times \$30 \text{ per hour} =$$

$$\$348,552 \text{ per year labor} / 24,593 \text{ total MSDS} =$$

$14.17 per MSDS

Let's extrapolate gross cost onto a theoretical company. Let's say that ACME Manufacturing needs 10,000 MSDSs to comply with OSHA and EPA standards and regulations across 25 locations. The company is likely spending between $120,000 to $160,000 per year in hard labor and material dollars for chemical information and related compliance management. Using this formula gives you a quick way to establish the approximate dollars being spent to manage chemical information.

NONTOXIC TIP

IF YOU ARE NOT SPENDING THIS KIND OF MONEY PER MSDS, YOU ARE SURELY EXPOSED AND HAVE BUILT UP CORPORATE LIABILITY AT A MUCH GREATER LEVEL.

It's simple to predict your company's MSDS management costs if you have an accurate count of the MSDSs used at each of your locations. The hard part is determining how many MSDSs you have. Roughly 85 percent of all hard copy MSDS binder systems are horribly out of date. Several factors contribute to incomplete MSDS binders:
- MSDSs have been removed from the binders and not returned
- MSDSs arrive from chemical manufacturers in numbers that make it difficult to pick out sheets that represent new products or legitimate revisions of existing MSDSs

- MSDSs may have either never arrived or have not been placed into their appropriate binders from the beginning

In short, the administration of the sheets is complicated. Job turnover is another big contributor. Joe or Sally gets promoted or transferred and MSDS management is assigned to a night shift employee who hasn't been trained; employers may claim "it will be a good learning experience," and an expensive one. Compliance is too often perceived as merely an unwanted cost of doing business. And besides, chances are that OSHA will not audit your operations—if you're lucky.

As we have indicated, MSDS automation and the resultant administrative savings recovers the initial investment and delivers an internally competitive ROI. Overall, only five percent of the chemical management dollar is spent in administration and reporting. Obviously larger savings are available in other key management functions like inventory management, collection, and disposal. Let's talk about how you might go about exploring potential savings and, just as important, communicating the opportunity to your organization.

NONTOXIC TIP

THE BIG DOLLARS ARE IN YOUR CHEMICAL REDUCTION EFFORTS.

CHEMICAL REDUCTION

The most documented chemical reduction programs have their origins in chemical supply chain management, with a focus on optimizing procurement. CSTCM programs deliver outcomes similar to supply chain management initiatives. It follows that any organization that is spending money on chemical compliance can establish a high-margin, high-return chemical management program for a few dollars more.

CSTCM implementation begins with chemical approval protocols. These approval filters severely curtail or eliminate the procurement of products containing hazardous chemical ingredients, which in turn may generate excessively costly hazardous waste. The working-capital impact associated with chemical inventory reductions can be phenomenal when chemical approval identifies:

• Chemicals that can be used across many sites

• Hazardous constituents (ingredients)

• Possible substitution chemicals for certain applications

• Candidates for a banned substances list

• Standard operating procedures to be applied toward chemical use

• Limitation on the number of certified vendors and approved chemicals

• Maximum inventory levels

NONTOXIC TIP

THE FIRST STEP IN GOOD RISK MANAGEMENT IS TO ELIMINATE THE RISK, WHICH YOU CAN DO WELL BY IMPLEMENTING A COMPREHENSIVE CHEMICAL APPROVAL PROCESS.

Reducing chemical inventories to improve business performance is not new. What I am suggesting is that compliance managers and the CEOs of small, mid-size, and even larger decentralized companies should bring their compliance minds into the business mainstream. Hazardous chemical management *will* reduce chemical inventories to your benefit. Let's review some chemical reduction success stories.

Supply-Side Chemical Reduction Example No. 1

In 1995 recommendations from the Duke Power commodity team resulted in significant chemical inventory reductions and cost savings for that energy company. During that year, Duke eliminated *560 chemicals* from its inventory. By optimizing the process of buying and using a variety of important commodities the company saved $22 million.

Duke continues to save money by replacing some chemicals and using all chemicals more efficiently. For example, the recommendations from the Solvents and Degreasers Commodity Team alone saved the company $1 million and reduced the amount of hazardous waste generated by 65,000 pounds each year, enhanced compliance with EPA and OSHA regulations, and reduced the use of aerosols.

Supply-Side Chemical Reduction Example No. 2

The private nonprofit group Chemical Strategies Partnerships (CSP) is doing some of the best work in this arena. Its programs recognize a need to shift procurement focus from material cost to chemical life-cycle costs. In such a program, one key vendor is generally selected and paired in partnership with the company through common objectives/incentives to achieve chemical reduction, reduce waste, and lower overall chemical costs. Assisted by CSP:

• General Motors implemented a chemical control program in 90 percent of its operations worldwide. It was able to reduce chemical use and cost by 30 percent. Affiliated environmental benefits included reduction in the number of chemicals, reduction in the amount of chemicals used, elimination of certain chemicals, and reduction in the complexity of the chemicals used.

• In the first three years of a supply-side program at a semiconductor facility, on-site chemical inventories were cut in half and volumes of chemicals used were also reduced by 50 percent over a two-year period. Hazardous wastes were reduced by 8 percent. Less hazardous chemicals were substituted and different container sizes were utilized for an additional savings of approximately $200,000 per year at a single facility.

Over the past 25 years, 3M's 3P Program reduced the company's waste by more than 800,000 tons with savings exceeding $825 million. These savings were achieved by *reducing* the use of organic solvents.

NONTOXIC TIP

CHEMICAL REDUCTION—IN CHEMICAL PRODUCT COUNT AND OVERALL VOLUME—CAN AFFECT THE SAME SAVINGS AND YIELD HEALTH AND SAFETY, ENVIRONMENTAL, AND LIABILITY AVOIDANCE BENEFITS, REGARDLESS OF WHETHER YOU APPROACH YOUR SAVINGS FROM THE SUPPLY OR COMPLIANCE SIDE OF THE EQUATION.

CSTCM Reduction Example

A CSTCM project in one of the world's top five forest products companies delivered similar results by implementing a chemical management and reduction program.

Coming entirely from the compliance side, this international giant:

- Cleaned the shelves of obsolete products
- Eliminated aerosols
- Avoided partially used containers
- Purchased smaller quantities
- Consolidated purchasing opportunities where product overlap between locations had been 8 percent

The results: a 70 percent reduction in chemical inventories with a similar reduction in waste generated. Also, product usage overlap between facilities rose to 60 percent.

Using compliance dollars and interdepartmental management techniques, the company achieved results almost identical to the larger manufacturing supply chain management programs. And it has saved millions of dollars to date through this integrated compliance-side effort.

CALCULATING FINANCIAL RETURNS

Start your calculations with the money you saved via automation of your MSDSs (using the formulas given earlier in this chapter) and add those savings to those you are about to project for your chemical reduction efforts. Keep in mind that the purchase price is only 10 to 50 percent of the total costs of using, controlling, and disposing of chemicals. Therefore, to calculate the rough impact of chemical reduction across your operations, measure as closely as possible the value of your current chemical inventory. Multiply your inventory value by a factor of two (conservative) to as high as 10 to account for the other life cycle elements besides purchase price. Then multiply by the percent of chemical inventory reduction you expect to achieve.

As an example, picture leading your EHS efforts over 25 similar manufacturing locations with an approximate chemical inventory value of $500,000 at each site. You estimate that the purchase price of your chemical inventory is only 25 percent of the total life cycle cost of using chemicals at the 25 sites. The total life cycle costs of chemical usage over the 25 sites would be $50 million (25 sites × $500,000 × 4). A 20 percent reduction in chemical inventory usage would save the organization $10 million each year.

You may want to adapt this approach to estimate the potential CSTCM savings in your operations. But note that every business is different and inventory reductions can range from 10 percent on the low side to more than 70 percent.

In order to generate and gain an approval of a formal AFE, considerably more work will be needed to project savings and ROI. In most cases a single site will be selected for a pilot program and specific due diligence will be conducted, which will involve evaluations such as a physical inventory, vendor/product cross-referencing, and hazardous ingredient determinations. All of these audits should be possible with any third-party vendor program you select and should be do-able within a hazardous chemical compliance budget and funds allocated for software tools and consulting.

What you will be able to achieve will vary widely depending on the historic site or corporate-level purchasing practices, the predisposition toward projects from headquarters, acceptance of a compliance platform by leadership, and your ability to generate resources for an integrated program.

If you do your homework, the financial improvements will be clear enough to launch a pilot site. They should also be significant enough to mandate senior management's attention and raise the probability of an enterprise-wide application of CSTCM.

REVIEW OF FINANCIAL COMPONENTS FOR DECISION MAKERS

Before we leave the topic of building your business case, here is a summary of the CSTCM business case cost and cost-reduction elements you should consider.

Elements of CSTCM Cost

Compliance-Based Data

You may already have everything you need from your own MSDS database or you may need to add additional information such as ingredients (chemical constituents). Your chemical data is at the very core of your CSTCM program. It will show you where you waste the most, where you risk the most, and where you have the most to gain. This data is probably not visible through any other information system at your company.

Analysis Tools

The key to unlocking the valuable secrets of your MSDS data will be the software that fits your company's needs. The tools you choose will help you analyze the data to answer the what, where, and how much questions relative to your chemicals. The ability to measure your data is critical.

Time

Internal company resources and possibly external expertise will be needed to plan, implement, and maintain your program. The better the analysis tools and data, the less people resources required for the desired detoxification effect; however, don't overlook this important cost when building your business case. Training and ongoing coordination will take time and effort that must be quantified for your business case to be credible.

Elements of CSTCM Cost Reductions

The cost reductions are the source of the profits that I have promised you. Here are the general areas of cost reduction that you should plan for and include in your business case for investing in CSTCM.

Data Automation

If you have not already done so, simply automating your MSDS management can be a source of cost reduction that can quickly pay for itself and provide savings into the future. We will use OSHA's MSDS annual handling cost estimate of $12.60 per MSDS. Let's take a mid-size MSDS database of 10,000 items spread over ten sites. That's a potential $126,000 in labor savings that may be redeployed to more productive activities ($126,000 over ten sites may not result in any headcount reduction).

Reduction in the Number of Different Chemicals Used

The high level of chemical purchasing redundancy noted in the case study in chapter 1 is common. Once this has been demonstrated by your chemical data, the work of cutting unnecessary purchases can begin almost immediately. As materials are purchased more efficiently, transaction or procurement costs are reduced. Early adopters of better chemical management have realized chemical inventory reductions of 10 percent to 70 percent. Let's assume a 40 percent reduction and average transaction costs of $100 per transaction (price negotiation, purchase order preparation, etc.) and that the chemical inventory turns over only once a year. If only half of that reduction is realized in the first year, $200,000 in purchasing costs could be eliminated or redeployed. Similar savings will result from a reduction in Stock Keeping Units (SKUs) and the administrative time that it takes to maintain these items in the company's inventory system.

Inventory Reductions and Cash

How would you like to free up some working capital? Take our assumed inventory reduction of 40 percent (half of it in year one) and apply that to the value of the chemical inventory. If 10,000 MSDSs over ten sites represents $10 million, that's $2 million of cash that won't be sitting on the shelves in the form of chemical inventory. You may want to place a value on these savings using your company's cost of capital or a planned rate of return on an alternative investment within the company. Let's say we can earn a modest 10 percent with our newly liberated working capital. That gives you a savings of $200,000 from the first year of your CSTCM program.

Vendor Consolidation

Your compliance-based data will show you how many items you purchase from multiple vendors. You will then be able to use this knowledge to consolidate your purchases and your purchasing power. By trimming the number of vendors and consolidating purchases on even a portion of your inventory, price discounting based on higher volume purchases will provide a lower cost of purchases. For example, if you realized an average price reduction of 5 percent on half of your purchases using the assumed quantities above, the savings potential is $250,000 (before factoring in reduced levels of inventory).

Regulatory Reporting

An important element of your CSTCM plan will be to limit the presence of the more dangerous chemicals. Not only will this reduce the occurrence of costly environmental messes and safety incidents but it will also reduce the burden of reporting items that appear on lists of regulated materials. The average estimated time to track and prepare reports on reportable constituents is 38 hours per year. Multiply the number of EPA reportable constituents (say, ten per site) by 38, then by a loaded labor rate ($50/hour). If these items could be reduced by even 25 percent, you could save $38,000 per year.

Waste Disposal Costs

Less inventory means less waste at the end. Multiply your hazardous waste disposal costs by your targeted reductions in chemical inventories for an idea of the savings that will come from lower waste disposal expense.

The potential savings are as real as they are significant. Now I hope you can see clearly how you can achieve greater profits while creating a safer, more environmentally friendly operation. That's the information you will want to communicate within your company to build that rock-solid business case.

CHAPTER 3

TELLING THE WORLD YOUR SUCCESS STORY

The oldest, most-told joke about the media goes back probably to before the 20th century. In essence, it goes like this: "It doesn't matter what they say about you in the newspapers as long as they spell your name right."

Nothing could be further from the truth. If you are a toxic CEO and the media reports negatively on your toxicity, they can spell your name right until the cows come home and it can still spell disaster for you and your company. The only way to get good press in the world of chemical management is to do the right thing and then be very careful about how you tell people about all the good things you've done.

THE BRAVE NEW WORLD OF PUBLIC RESPONSIBILITY

Some corporate leaders back in the '40s, '50s, and '60s went out of their ways to ensure that people and the planet were well cared for. But in those good old days company officials who devoted time and money to protect human and environmental health were usually acting out of some deep-rooted personal convictions. Nobody was forcing them to be socially responsible. The Feds didn't demand compliance. The media didn't regularly report on who dumped what chemical in which river.

Today it's a new ball game. It has been more than 20 years since the first Earth Day and nobody is in doubt of the definitions of common terms such as "environmental pollution" or "toxic chemical." We now live in a world where corporate social responsibility is *expected*. And the bad guys get their names spelled—correctly, or incorrectly—in newspapers and magazines, and on the Internet and television.

PEOPLE CARE ABOUT WHAT YOU DO

In a massive, worldwide "millennium poll" conducted in 1999 under the auspices of the Conference Board of New York and the Prince of Wales Business Leaders Forum in London, 25,000 people were surveyed on their feelings about modern corporate responsibility. Check out these results:

- 90 percent of the people surveyed said they wanted companies to focus on more than profitability

- 60 percent said they would put corporate citizenship ahead of brand reputation in forming impressions of companies

- 40 percent said they responded or talked negatively about companies they thought were not acting in a socially responsible manner

- 17 percent said they avoided the products of companies they thought were not socially responsible

In other words, people do care about what you do, and they expect the media and the watchdog groups to keep them posted on what you are doing. When hazardous chemicals are involved in your operations, people tend to get even more interested because there's been so much negative publicity about chemicals in the past few decades.

Recent years have been filled with examples of companies that have felt the brunt of the media's scorn concerning corporate mishandling of hazardous chemicals and misinformation being spread via corporate public relations. For instance, the media criticized the following:

- A major cement manufacturer for promoting sustainable development at the same time its plants were being fined by environmental regulators for exceeding emissions limitations

- Chemical companies for running PR campaigns against replacing CFCs with the more benign hydrochlorofluorocarbons (HCFCs)

- A chemical manufacturer for its PR efforts to label the toxic herbicide paraquat as "environmentally friendly"

- Several companies for disguising damaging information about vinyl chloride, one of the most potent sources of dioxin

NONTOXIC TIP

ALONG WITH TODAY'S INCREASED SCRUTINY OF HOW CORPORATIONS CONDUCT BUSINESS COMES A BIG DOSE OF SKEPTICISM FOR ALMOST ANY COMPANY'S CLAIMS OF ENVIRONMENTAL RESPONSIBILITY.

With so much talk flying around today about corporate greed, some people will naturally be suspicious. It stands to reason that if your company does spend the effort and money to do something remarkably responsible, it ought to earn some bragging rights. Unfortunately, that is only true in theory. In today's climate, merely communicating your story about some "right thing" your company has done is no guarantee you'll win friends and influence people.

MAKE SURE TO WALK YOUR TALK

One recent report by the corporate oversight group PR Watch entitled "Flack Attack" complained that "corporate responsibility is all too frequently mere PR designed to reassure the public, when in reality very little has changed." Journalists and watchdog groups frequently brand company officials and publicists as "greenwashers" who engage in disinformation so as to present an environmentally responsible public image. ("Greenwash" is a hybrid of the environmentalist term "green" and the old pejorative "whitewash"). These same journalists, watchdogs, and vocal private citizens demand that companies walk their talk—meaning that if you're going to say you did something socially responsible, it had darn well better be so.

What's at stake, of course, is only everything: customer, stakeholder, shareholder, and even regulator attitudes toward your company. Your company reputation may be damaged by corporate PR that is inaccurate, spun the wrong way, or downright false. That will translate directly and negatively to your bottom line. It will be up to you and your publicity people to make sure that the story your company tells about your CSTCM program is accurate and true. In some cases, it may be necessary for corporate legal counsel to render an opinion on one or more of your company's socially responsible actions before you are able to publicize anything. For instance, some green claims are required to meet federal agency definitions—such as the EPA's definition of terms such as "recycled" and "recyclable."

It is unquestionable that good, socially responsible CSTCM actions can be huge PR bonuses for your company, and they can make you, your employees, and shareholders justifiably proud.

A POSITIVE PR CASE STUDY

A perfect example of a company that has received good pollution prevention press is 3M. Back in 1975, 3M adopted what may be the country's first global environmental policy. The same year, the company introduced the voluntary 3P program. Both initiatives gained the company positive publicity.

As noted in chapter 2, by the year 2001, 3M had prevented releases of more than 800,000 tons of pollutant and realized a savings of more than $825 million. According to the company, it continues to improve compliance assurance systems every year to meet and exceed government and 3M standards. And the company, like most savvy corporate entities, sends out media releases reporting its responsible actions.

Not surprisingly, 3M received a lot of deserved mileage out of being named the recipient of Keep America Beautiful, Inc.'s "Vision for America Award" in 2002. 3M CEO W. James McNerney, Jr. must have felt justifiably proud walking up to the podium at New York City's Grand Hyatt Hotel to receive the award for all the 3M employees who had worked so hard on the company's Environmental Management Systems over almost a quarter century.

But merely doing right things won't guarantee positive publicity and an improved reputation for your chemical management victories. To help you cover your bases, here are some time-honored strategies for telling your story to maximum benefit.

TELL YOUR STORY INTERNALLY

The first order of business in telling your story is making sure that your employees know what you are trying to do, what you've accomplished, and what you will continue to do with CSTCM.

From the outset of your CSTCM program, it is vitally important that you have the support of your own employees and shareholders. Employees and shareholders care about their company's reputation. Staff morale can be enhanced greatly when you do the right thing, but in order for those good feelings to grow, you have to water them with internal information about what's going on with your chemical management program and the benefits it will yield. Managers and team members must know the story of the good work they are doing and be able to communicate it to their coworkers. Company newsletters, bulletin boards, Intranet postings, regular meetings, and awards ceremonies are excellent opportunities to spread the good word and build inspiration. When people are armed with positive information, they are empowered to scale even greater heights.

TELL YOUR STORY TO YOUR COMMUNITY AND THE WORLD

You may oversee a large corporation with a well-staffed PR department or you may be a small company with few resources or people devoted to spreading the good word about your company. Whichever the case, the basic rules of approaching the media are the same. The most effective way to generate publicity is to establish respectful, professional relationships with newspeople. It's like being a good salesman. The clients with whom you have a positive relationship will be better, long-term clients than those to whom you merely sell products and services. As a well-informed and responsible business leader, you should establish several news contacts in different mediums in your community. The legitimizing effect of press attention can put your company's products and services at the top of the list. *Media attention can equal credibility.*

Journalism is a high-stress job, with seemingly endless deadline pressures. Just as people in your company do, media professionals often feel like they are buried in work. Because they are required to supply the public with information in a sea of content that includes newspapers, magazines, radio, 24-hour TV broadcasts, and the Internet, journalists everywhere are under even greater pressure to produce more news faster.

NONTOXIC TIP

IN MANY WAYS, WORKING WITH THE MEDIA IS NOT MUCH DIFFERENT THAN WORKING WITH CHEMICALS IN YOUR OPERATION. RESPECT THEM AND HONOR THEIR POSITIVE POTENTIAL, AND THE BENEFITS CAN BE GREAT. TREAT THEM CASUALLY AND WITH NO RESPECT AND THEY CAN HURT YOU.

CREATE GOOD MEDIA RELEASES

Don't kid yourself that editors are waiting for you to bring them your good news. Business, environmental, and news editors receive thousands of press releases a year, as do assignment desk people at television and radio stations.

Don't pester newspeople or be a publicity hound. Alerting the media to your CSTCM success stories is not unlike selling your products or services. Only sell stories that are truly solid news. You lose credibility every time you bother the media with a story that is weak or not a story at all. And the only way you can know if your story has value is by carefully reading your selected newspapers, magazines, and trade publications, watching television, and listening to the radio to see and hear what actually constitutes valid newsworthiness. Not everything you do in CSTCM will be newsworthy!

N O N T O X I C   T I P

IF YOU ARE ABLE TO GIVE EDITORS AND REPORTERS TIMELY IDEAS WITH REAL, SOLID, POSITIVE NEWS VALUE, YOU CAN BECOME RESPECTED AS A NEWS SOURCE IN THEIR EYES.

Be considerate of the type of news a particular news organization likes to report and pitch your story to that specific angle. If you are pitching your story to an environmental magazine, the environment comes first. In a health-and-safety trade magazine arena, you'd want your story to focus on worker safety. Business sections of newspapers, business journal-type publications, and trade magazines and newsletters offer you exposure with highly targeted audiences, which is particularly important if you are working business-to-business (B2B). Use common sense in finding story angles for specific media outlets.

Creating good media releases requires thorough knowledge of what the media expects you to give them. It's not rocket science; it's a time-honored process. Here are some keys to good media releases:

- Understand what your real, simple message is
- Make sure you have real news to report
- Make headlines clear, emotionally interesting, and different

- Convey your message in the headline, subhead, and first few sentences
- Always include the "five Ws" (who, what, when, where, and why)
- Supply good quotes from people in authority at your company
- Don't get too technical; keep it simple!
- Keep numbers simple and understandable
- Check your facts (you're the expert in chemical management, not the journalist)
- Always provide the news story release date ("for immediate release" is common)
- Always provide a contact name, telephone number, and/or e-mail address

You may feel that you have several interesting elements to your company's news story, but the media release should sell only one. Greater detail can be supplied and background information can be given to journalists as separate attachments or in private interviews outside of a news event setting.

You can send out hard copy media releases, but check to see if the news organization receives or even prefers electronic media releases. If you have good photographs to include with your release—and they legitimately apply to your story—see how the journalist prefers to receive them (physically or electronically). If journalists are coming out to your location, inform them in advance of good photo opportunities.

If you have access to related industry studies on chemical use/disposal and pollution prevention or if you have government reports and public surveys that are beneficial in telling your company's CSTCM story, let the journalist know you can provide them. Journalists very much want to have too much background information rather than not enough.

Finally, don't disregard the opportunity to reformat the same good CSTCM story for different outlets. You may be able to get your story in the morning newspaper, on the evening news, on a televised news-magazine or morning news program, in trade publications, on Web sites, and more. Your story may only be local or, if your company is large, it may warrant national or even international coverage.

MEDIA EVENTS

Staging a good media event is harder than merely sending out a media release. And in doing media events you have to be equally, or even more careful that what you are selling is newsworthy. The media spends a lot of money and labor to send reporters, photographers, and camerapeople out to your facility or event location. You had better make the story worth all that effort and attention. One thing you do not want to do is come off looking like your event is too staged. The event must be well planned and executed, and this kind of polish can only come through pre-event practice.

When dealing with the broadcast media (radio and TV), it is equally important to try to find emotional or human interest angles to your story. When you supply the broadcast media with interviews and sound bites, try to restrict your response to ten seconds of content, time yourself when practicing what you are going to say. It helps to make those ten seconds about emotional subjects, though you shouldn't get emotional! Don't be afraid to repeat yourself often in an interview. Sometimes people, even journalists, need to hear something more than once. And in a broadcast interview, you may say something a little better the second time, giving the editor a chance to use the better take.

For corporate executives and employees who will be interviewed by the broadcast media, it helps to practice in front of a video camera beforehand, to smooth out the rough edges in the performance before the media arrives. Of course, for major corporations and national stories, using a media coach is not a bad idea. Such consultants exist and many of them are former journalists or on-screen talent themselves.

By and large, media events should be held in the morning, to honor media deadlines and give the journalists, editors, and news anchors time to prepare their stories for public consumption. Sometimes, whether your story is featured or not will depend more on how busy the journalists are when you contact them than on how great your story is. If you have professionally shot video of your company or of a particular element of your chemical management program, be sure to let television assignment editors or journalists know you are willing to supply the video (though they often want to shoot their own). If reporters can't come to your workplace, offer to go to the journalist's office or newspaper, magazine, TV, or radio station.

Finally, there are some special applications through which you may also receive helpful media coverage. Some Internet sites will allow you to register with them as an expert, and journalists frequently rely on these industry-focused experts to find people to quote or businesses to feature in stories. Another avenue to draw attention to your CSTCM work may be through the writing of an article for a trade magazine or even a piece for your local newspaper's Op-Ed pages.

IF THE MEDIA GETS FACTS WRONG

If the media makes a mistake in reporting about your company, don't fly off the handle. Your job is to help the media report accurate information. When errors in reporting your story appear in print or on radio, TV, or the Web:

- Call the station or office immediately and politely explain what was reported inaccurately
- Ask for a correction
- Ask that assignment desk editors who may pick up the story are notified
- Alert other media outlets who may pick up the story of the misinformation

When doing damage control it is important not to disparage the media because media outlets often rely on other media for story ideas. Your story may get repeated with little effort on your part, and you want to make sure positive and accurate information is going out to the public.

JOURNALISTS DECIDE WHAT'S NEWS, NOT YOU

The journalist and the news organization management are the gatekeepers of public information. The media decides what gets printed in the newspapers and magazines and what airs on radio, TV, or even Web sites such as CNN.com and other respected online services. If you are careful to ensure that your news is different from the run-of-the-mill stories we see and hear every day, you will increase your chances of play in the media. Likewise, if you find a way to appeal to emotions, you'll have a better chance of getting good publicity. Everyone responds to an emotional story, including journalists and editors.

News about chemical management is somewhat unique. CSTCM and its benefits to people and the planet are a niche story you don't see every day. That can be good. Not that many companies effectively reduce the amount of hazardous chemicals they use, store, and dispose of. Nor do you hear every day about a company that spends a lot of its precious resources on making sure that their people and planet are safer. And it's likely that your competitors won't be doing what you're doing.

As long as you get your facts right and approach the media in the proper manner, you have every right to get your good story out to the public. Remember, you want to have a good, professional relationship with the media based on mutual respect. If a reporter or photographer does a particularly good job on your story, there is nothing wrong with sending him or her a letter of thanks and a courtesy copy to the managing editor or news director. As long as you are legitimately thanking someone for doing an outstanding job and as long as you do not unduly flatter the journalist, you have every right to simply say thank you. After all, if they select you and your story among the many others in competition for space, that is a noteworthy achievement in its own right.

Finally, never forget that your job as a nontoxic CEO is to use every means at your disposal, including good publicity, to ensure that people are inspired to maintain your company's social responsibilities.

CEO's AFTERWORD:
NONTOXIC LEADERSHIP AFTER 9/11

Hopefully, the subtitle of this book—*Protecting Your People, Planet, and Profits Through Better Chemical Management*—indicates everything you want to do in becoming a more responsible member of the chemical-use and -management business community. But since September 11, 2001, and the search for weapons of mass destruction in Iraq, people everywhere, not the least of them CEOs, have been shocked into thinking about ways to prevent terrorism and protect our loved ones (and yes, our workers, customers, environment, and businesses) from the unimaginable actions of a few misguided zealots.

At the risk of oversimplifying a very complex topic, there are essentially three levels of reactions prompted by the 9/11 attacks:

1. Preventing attacks: border security and intelligence gathering

2. Elimination of threats: covert and overt military and intelligence actions

3. Emergency preparedness: local, state, and federal interagency cooperation

At the time of this book's publication, the U.S. government and its Office of Homeland Security seemed to be doing a pretty good job in the three arenas identified above. But we are clearly living in different times. Our world has been inexorably changed. So how do you prepare for a new, less kind-and-gentle millennium? One thing you must do is ask questions!

What is a weapon?
What can be turned against us?
Where are we vulnerable?
What can we do to prepare?
What can be—and needs to be—changed in my company's operations?

There is a fourth level of reaction to 9/11 that should be considered by American businesses that deal with hazardous chemicals: risk minimization or reducing access to chemical weapons.

Companies with large amounts of high-risk chemical products, like bulk chlorine, gasoline, and nuclear wastes, have probably already taken steps to beef up their security and facility protection procedures. It may be that most of the obvious targets are the most secure and the least of our worries. What we may have to worry about more in the future are the thousands of chemicals that are stored at much less secure locations around the country—some in our own neighborhoods. After all, any significant stockpile of toxins and potentially hazardous chemicals at any business location throughout the country might become a target for terrorists.

Terrorist attacks that may occur among us may not be on the same level as those we witnessed on 9/11; however, we have learned that we need to think unconventionally and more thoroughly about risk and risk mitigation.

NONTOXIC TIP

IN LIGHT OF POTENTIAL TERRORIST ACTIONS, NOW IS THE RIGHT TIME TO REVIEW ALL THE CHEMICAL PRODUCTS THAT ARE USED AND STORED THROUGHOUT YOUR OPERATIONS.

As a businessperson, you could be responsible for any catastrophic use of your chemical inventory that would put your company in great jeopardy, not to mention the threat to the health and safety of your surrounding community.

The good news is, something can be done to provide us with greater security. Some businesses have large inventories of chemicals they simply don't need. Those companies could reduce, or in some cases eliminate, stores of these chemicals. Some chemicals are outdated; some are duplicates of others. In some instances, more environmentally and medically benign alternatives exist.

New technologies provide us with the tools to manage our chemical inventories better. CSTCM can help you do your part for homeland security through control-oriented MSDS automation, better procurement, and chemical inventory tracking. By implementing a structured CSTCM program it is no exaggeration to say you will be doing your part to protect all of us.

Chemicals will continue to play a vitally important role in the economic stability of our country. But we can't escape the fact that those much-needed chemicals could pose a clear and present danger if turned against us.

TAKE ACTION NOW

Revisit how you are protecting your employees and our local communities from unexpected but *intentional* chemical release into our environment.

Take a fresh look at the types of chemical products you need to operate your business and reassess adequate inventory levels.

If you truly want to be a nontoxic CEO, ask questions, get information, and take action!

THE IMPLEMENTER'S WORKBOOK

CHAPTER 4

CREATING YOUR CSTCM BLUEPRINT

This chapter addresses CSTCM application and installation. Though the subject matter is dry, I have tried to interject helpful lists and analogies that will take you through the review of your existing system, the accumulation of data, and the process of using that data to reap savings.

Building a CSTCM system is much like the process of buying and moving into a home. It is obvious that all homes are not the same. There are condominiums, single-family dwellings, homes with acreage, and homes in compact subdivisions. Regardless of the abode, we go through a process to help us find the perfect "home sweet home." This usually starts with design objectives and ends in a list of amenities. We prioritize this list deciding what is most important and where we won't compromise.

CSTCM systems are similar. You may find that a small system accommodates your needs. You may decide to step into a small system that can grow with you. You may find that you have several sites that require the exact same method of controls. Whatever your needs, there is a logical set of steps and some very important guidelines that will help get your CSTCM house in order.

RAW MATERIALS: WHAT DO YOU NEED TO START TO BUILD

"I am rather like a mosquito in a nudist camp: I know what I want to do, but I don't know where to begin."—Stephen Bayne

We all have had this feeling when a job seems daunting. To get started we break the project down into small tasks. In a CSTCM project, the first task is to get the data. In order to analyze your chemical practices, you need to have data about your chemicals. It's plain and simple: if you have no data, you do not have the information you need to implement CSTCM. If we go back to our house analogy, you need to know the raw materials required to build it. The MSDSs and indexes are the raw materials.

> **NONTOXIC TIP**
>
> AT FIRST GLANCE, YOU MAY CONSIDER CHEMICAL MANAGEMENT A SMALL PERCENTAGE OF YOUR COMPANY'S MANAGEMENT CHORES AND A SMALL PIECE OF YOUR BOTTOM LINE. DON'T BE FOOLED! FOUR TO TEN PERCENT OF YOUR TOTAL PROCUREMENT PROGRAM CAN BE MOVED TO THE BOTTOM LINE THROUGH CSTCM. YOUR SAVINGS AND RISK REDUCTION CAN BE SIGNIFICANT.

CSTCM systems can be purchased turnkey, with data already converted and indexed. Your data is your company's asset and it had better be accurate. A small percentage of organizations opt to take the time and energy to do their own data entry. It cannot be overemphasized that the key to a good CSTCM program is the quality of the raw materials.

A hard copy MSDS is entered into the system as full text or as an image. MSDS images are typically represented as PDFs (Portable Document Format) files but can come in other formats such as TIFFs (Tagged Image File Format) files. It is possible to turn PDF images into text through Optical Character Recognition (OCR), but without human correction and quality control you will encounter text errors. If you are relying on uncorrected OCR for full-text searches, there will be many cases where the words are incorrect. The results of searches on OCR data cannot be trusted when someone has just spilled a caustic substance on his or her skin or splashed acetone in his or her eye. The inaccuracies in OCR data will frustrate users, possibly endanger the users, and may provide an excuse to not use your chemical management system. Again, it can potentially expose you to greater risk, which is not something a nontoxic CEO would want. Albert Einstein said, "Everything should be as simple as possible, but not simpler." Beware of low-cost "seems simple" solutions.

In replacing legacy MSDS management systems, my company has discovered that bad data can be expensively discarded because of its inferior quality. Image-based MSDSs are usually less expensive than text-based. Here is a warning: money saved on poor-quality MSDSs (the raw materials of your CSTCM system) will result in termites throughout the house. The data can be buggy and inaccurate.

FIGURE 12.

What is a "good" MSDS?

A good MSDS for any given chemical product provides health and safety information as well as environmental information. (See the Appendix for a facsimile of a typical MSDS.)
It typically contains:

- The constituent ingredients
- Constituent percentages found in the chemical
- Alternative names for the chemical
- Personal protective equipment (PPE)
- Hazardous Materials Information System (HMIS)
- National Fire Protection Association (NFPA) information
- Other enormously useful data

Often data is reformatted into a standard ANSI (American National Standards Institute) 16-section format to ensure a consistent appearance to the end user. The ultimate benefits of text-based MSDSs is that they are flexible and more accurately represent the chemical data that the manufacturer had intended. A text MSDS accomplishes this by offering nontoxic companies enhanced search capabilities and readability.

The downside of a full-text MSDS solution is its increased cost. A vendor with a rich master source of converted MSDSs can be cost-competitive when compared to image-based MSDS offerings. An image may be cheaper than text, but with its lessened readability it requires the extraction of key indexes into fields that are searchable. Although less of a problem today because of cheap disk capacity, the image files still require much more disk space.

NONTOXIC TIP

To know whether the data in your legacy system will be useful as a base for your new system, you must fully understand your existing data and unequivocally trust its quality.

The value of the data does not stop with the actual MSDS. The indexes that are created to help you pull the information out of the system are also important to CSTCM success.

Whoever converts your MSDSs should be able to provide many indexes to your MSDS data that will aid in implementing CSTCM. When interviewing an MSDS conversion vendor, your selected partner should be able to provide the following benefits to help enhance reporting:

- Ingredient and physical data info required for chemical reporting
- CAS and Compound Name for regulatory list-matching for Tier II, Form R, and other lists
- Product synonyms
- User-defined synonyms
- HMIS/NFPA hazard rating determinations
- Secondary chemical product labels
- Site locations where each chemical is being used
- Internal part numbers

Bill Gates, Microsoft CEO and author of the book *Business at the Speed of Thought,* supports the need for electronic data in daily business. Gates says, "Bringing together the right information with the right people will dramatically improve a company's ability to develop and act in strategic business opportunities." In order to match people and accurate data, high-quality MSDSs in electronic format are not a nicety; they're a necessity. Make sure that this is not taken lightly. If you cut corners on conversion, your house will not be in order.

BEST PRACTICE: GOING BEYOND THE OBVIOUS

"Simple, clear purpose and principles give rise to complex and intelligent behavior. Complex rules and regulations give rise to simple and stupid behavior."—Dee Hock

Best-practice processes will help you build a better system, if your policies are clear and precise. Best practices provide the blueprint for reducing chemicals in the workplace. You will also want to add company-specific policies to your best practices list. Don't forget the personalization of the best practice policy for each individual. You may be able to tie the best-practice policies into your company's or department's mission statement. If you can, do it! Below you will find a list of best practices you should incorporate into your plan.

1. Develop and validate a "do not use here" chemicals watch list. This is a list of chemicals that should not be used due to their dangerous nature or their potential for creating long-term harm to users and/or the environment.

2. Identify chemical product groupings or families. An example of these grouping are paints, solvents, adhesives, lubricants, etc.

3. Select approved chemicals and approved vendors for each chemical family.

4. Identify chemical product substitutions and an approved chemical list. This will help you determine which products can be safely substituted for those chemicals that are on the banned list.

5. Eliminate obsolete and out-of-date chemical products. For those partially used chemicals that are on the shelf, clean them up and get them off the shelves. This should be done every six months, and products must be disposed of properly.

6. Automate the materials requisition and approval process (which we will address later in this chapter). You will keep unwanted toxins from entering the site and consequently reduce risk because there will be fewer workplace and environmental exposures to chemicals.

NONTOXIC TIP

EACH PURCHASE IS NOT ABOUT "HOW CHEAP CAN WE GET IT" BUT HOW WE CAN PARTNER WITH A VENDOR TO ACHIEVE OUR DESIRED RESULTS AND MAXIMIZE OUR ECONOMIC RETURN.

EHS departments will enjoy never-before-experienced uniform compliance with OSHA regulations. This data benefit will include:

• Eliminating MSDS hard copy dependency

- Centralizing your database (Search-View-Print (SVP) will be accessible at all locations)
- Implementing a standard data-updating process
- 40 percent plus gross ROI on administrative costs and initial capital

Through your constituent-specific data, you will reduce the cost of accurate data gathering for your EPA Tier II and Form R reporting. That means weeks of labor saved per year for each reportable chemical.

Your best-practices actions will encourage the elimination of product redundancy, result in fewer vendors to manage, and provide increased purchasing leverage. On the process and maintenance side you will have identified fewer acceptable products that are approved for each task, which will keep unapproved chemicals off site. If the chemicals are not on site, you will also generate less waste, resulting in a huge economic impact. Also, overall compliance cost will drop because you are managing fewer chemicals.

NONTOXIC TIP

GOOD NEWS: CSTCM IS USHERING IN A NEW ERA OF INTEGRATED THINKING AND OPTIMIZATION, COMBINING THE FULFILLMENT OF YOUR COMPANY'S REGULATORY OBLIGATIONS WITH NEW SOCIAL AWARENESS, ECOLOGICAL PROTECTION, AND PROFITABILITY.

As a nontoxic CEO, you will appreciate that the data will enhance your emergency preparedness and training. Finally, administrative and operational savings will produce a better-than-hurdle-rate ROI.

Don't wait until everything is in place with a system to start best practices. The best practices include basic good housekeeping behaviors that you should be doing at your company now. Clean up your existing inventories, even while you are tackling the implementation of CSTCM, to ensure your safer and more profitable future as a nontoxic CEO.

CSTCM, in its simplest characterization, is source reduction. The fewer hazardous materials you have on hand, the fewer chemical risks you juggle and the less hazardous waste you generate. Just a little advice from past experience: don't neglect the simple fixes that your maintenance department can offer. Routinely inspecting and maintaining equipment can mean greater human and environmental safety and money savings. Instituting in-process recycling of hazardous materials in your production process may be appropriate; it's a method many companies find beneficial. Recirculating hazardous chemicals directly back into your production process can reduce or eliminate hazardous wastes and even increase end-product yield. Finally, only purchase what you need for the job and use it up! This is the one key to reducing hazardous chemical inventories.

REVIEW YOUR EXISTING FRAMEWORK

We've established the need for data. We have established best-practices policies. Now you will begin to audit current EHS practices to find out what you already have in place—both in processes and on-site materials. This audit will help you determine whether you can modify the existing system or if you need to scrap everything and build it from scratch.

Even our best systems will not last forever, and many simply do not keep up with the changing needs of a healthy organization and dynamic marketplace. The implementation of CSTCM is a perfect opportunity to look critically at your current EHS management methods; it's a golden opportunity for improvement.

NONTOXIC TIP

INCLUDING THE USERS AND THE OWNERS OF THE CURRENT SYSTEM IN YOUR AUDIT WILL HELP RELIEVE ANY POSSIBLE ANXIETIES AND HELP YOU ENSURE COOPERATION.

Your chemical management systems may be electronic or manual, formal or informal. The details don't matter. It's critical to understand and evaluate your current systems to plan current and future objectives. The results will give you much needed insight into:

- The relationship between existing systems
- How data/information is developed and validated
- The owners of the systems

- The political stakeholders
- Turf issues that may arise

Sources of EHS data can be found throughout your organization. Almost every major department uses or generates some type of EHS data. To determine the state of chemical management in your organization today, the first step is to break down the current systems into broad categories and analyze the interaction between the various systems. For example, you can look at your organization in terms of systems that are required for:

- Chemical management
- Process management
- Environmental management
- Customer management

A review of these systems will produce necessary information needed to prepare your request for funds. Cross-linkages between systems and data sharing needs are information vendors will require in preparing a complete RFP response.

NONTOXIC TIP

A QUALITY SOFTWARE SOLUTION SHOULD PROVIDE FOR ENTERPRISE-WIDE MANAGEMENT WHILE SIMULTANEOUSLY ALLOWING FOR SITE-SPECIFIC DATA COLLECTION AND MANAGEMENT.

DEFINING THE SCALE OF THE PROJECT

You now decide whether your CSTCM system will be installed on a site-by-site basis or on a broader, enterprise-wide approach.

Site-by-site solutions allow more autonomy and may be easier to sell to management due to a reduced cost if only a few sites buy in. That said, from an organizational perspective it's much more difficult to implement CSTCM one site at a time. But in some organizations, you may have to walk before you run.

An enterprise solution offers economies of scale, one voice for the organization, one source of data, software version control, and many other positive attributes; however, it inherently generates more organizational politics and the "Big Brother's telling us what to do" syndrome. Obviously, there are organizational pros and cons to either solution.

You'll want to select a system that will help you control inventory, control chemical purchases, manage chemical use, and manage chemical disposal. These are the four control points that will allow you to reduce dangerous chemical inventories, save money on purchases, assure the right chemicals are used for the right tasks, and reduce waste disposal costs.

Note: You should compare the results of the in-house audit with the list of features that you want in your CSTCM system. At this point you are not trying to hammer out every detail of your program; only identify the main system features and intended audience.

Your requirements document should include:

1. Introduction and description of the project.
   a. *Why is the project necessary?*
   Who is the intended audience? Address the users' needs as well as management's concern for ROI. It is imperative that you can show a solid business case for undertaking this project, as discussed in chapter 2.

2. Features of the project.
   a. *What does the project look like?*
   List the main features of the desired system along with enough detail so that someone who is not intimately familiar with the project will understand.

   b. *How does your project interface with existing legacy systems or proposed systems?*
   Describe the interfaces that will be necessary to integrate existing systems with the proposed system.

   c. *What are the IT requirements?*
   Describe the anticipated software, hardware, and networking requirements necessary for this project. For example, a vendor-hosted MSDS system would require Web access to the vendor's site.

d. *What are other project requirements?*
Don't forget to take into consideration training, installation, and ongoing support.

Your requirements document must be correctly stated and unambiguous. This document will be enhanced to create the RFP for vendors. It's OK to do some dreaming at this point. You can prioritize your requirements later, so long as they are truly necessary for the project. Just be careful that your requirements are complete. The requirements document is often used to seek initial funding from management, so make it good.

CREATING THE REQUEST FOR PROPOSAL

You have already gathered a good set of specifications with the requirements document. Now you only need to turn your requirements into a series of questions to the various vendors. Again, this should be done in a collaborative effort with all the members of the CSTCM committee.

Since verbal communication between the committee and the prospective vendors is usually not allowed, you must ensure your RFP has open-ended questions that will illicit complete responses. Vendors tend to overstate their products' capabilities, and sometimes their salespeople may be unaware of the current features of their products or soon-to-be-released features.

It is enormously helpful to ask very specific questions that require thoughtful, well-researched responses. For example, below you will find a few sample RFP-specific questions to ask regarding interest in Tier II reporting.

Sample Tier II-Specific Vendor RFP Questions

- *Does the software provide the federal form, a state-specific form, or just a worksheet?*
- *Are the necessary forms provided as a service by the vendor or through software that you can access?*
- *How is inventory imported into the system?*
- *Does the software support product and location exemptions?*

SYSTEM DESIGN AND TECHNOLOGY

Once you have stated your objectives and created prioritized requirements, you will be ready to find a CSTCM system that will work for you. There are many different systems available that can handle some form of chemical management. Allow vendors to propose their best solution for your company. Here is where you will really see if they understand your needs.

In CSTCM we are concerned with applications that help manage chemicals through the cradle-to-grave process—the continuum that follows a chemical in your organization from formal chemical request and approval to the end when the chemical is used or disposed of. It is a specific managerial progression.

Many organizations rely on ERP systems such as Baan, J. D. Edwards, Oracle, SAP, or PeopleSoft for numerous organizational functions. You will have to determine whether a large ERP system can actually handle CSTCM functions. ERP systems focus primarily on central stores purchasing and inventory or material and vendor management. They typically do not meet the needs of CSTCM since they are not primarily chemical in focus. Or, you may opt for one of the numerous available "best of breed" applications designed to handle specific aspects of CSTCM, but not designed to deal with purchasing and inventory in general.

As you design your CSTCM system, you will have to decide whether you want to install the new system in house or whether it would be cheaper and easier for the vendor to do the hosting. Of course, the Internet has provided an anytime/anywhere connection that makes it easily feasible to have someone else host your solution. But let's first look at what it would actually take to host the new system in house. To evaluate in-house hosting, you will want to ask yourself some key questions, such as those in the self-hosting questions box (see Figure 13).

NONTOXIC TIP

MANY OF THE STEPS AND PITFALLS IN IMPLEMENTATION CAN USUALLY BE AVOIDED THROUGH THE USE OF AN ASP.

FIGURE 13.

Self-Hosting Questions Checklist

- ❑ Do we have the infrastructure to guarantee 24/7 uptime for this application?
- ❑ When can our IT shop install and test the new application and move it into production ?
- ❑ Does IT's timeframe match the company's CSTCM project timeline?
- ❑ How does hosting this application fit into our core business?
- ❑ Is hosting our own TCM system honestly do-able?
- ❑ Will we face turf/political issues such as which server the application resides on?
- ❑ Who will pay for the hardware, operating system, and database licensing?
- ❑ How will new software version rollouts be handled?
- ❑ What will be the timing of new version rollouts?
- ❑ Will in-house IT want to test new version functions/compatibility on test servers?
- ❑ How long will IT testing take?
- ❑ What are the cost transfers to my department?
- ❑ Who will install data as the vendor continuously provides new MSDSs and related data?
- ❑ Does the vendor's choice of operating system/development tools/database meet our standards?
- ❑ As we migrate new standards, will the vendor's system still meet our standards?
- ❑ If we are slow to move to new systems/databases, how long will the vendor support the older standards?

Finally, you will want to consider the cost of ownership. When you purchase licenses to host software, there is normally a software maintenance service agreement that provides the vendor with the funds to cover upgrades to the software and provide technical support.

Your CSTCM system can be hosted as an ASP solution. In this scenario, you typically do not license the software and you normally have a monthly fee that includes the leasing of the software as well as the fees covering the hosting costs.

In the ASP model, you avoid initial large cash outlays because you don't purchase software licenses. In this case there is no software maintenance agreement, and depending upon the terms of your ASP contract, you can drop the use of the system without costly consequences. The downside of an ASP is that your Total Cost of Ownership (TCO) may be higher in the long term, so it is important to decide if short-term preservation of capital is more important than long-term TCO. You will also have to deal with IT security issues.

Positive attributes of the ASP model include:
- TCM software design, hosting, and networking are vendor core competencies
- New software releases and MSDS updates that are available immediately without your IT department's involvement
- Avoiding political issues within your own organization, stealing resources
- Immediate data updating

Since this is a mission-critical application, the application must be available 24/7. The only way that this can happen is if the ASP vendor has some failover procedures and has a location or a co-location where there is redundancy in every aspect of the hosted application. That means assurance of redundant power sources, servers, air temperature controls, ventilation systems, and several Internet backbone connections through several telecommunication companies. Since your data is totally under the ASP vendor's control, you will want to make sure that you fully understand the services the vendor will provide.

You will want a service level agreement between your company and the vendor. It should cover topics such as:

- Methodology for how your data access will be limited to authorized users
- The agreed-upon service level and remedies
- Data backup procedures
- Pricing and payment terms
- Dispute resolution and termination clauses
- Security and confidentiality
- Data ownership defined
- Data security defined

As you can see, the ASP model is attractive since it provides anywhere/anytime access and allows your company to concentrate on its key business strengths. A good business-case feature nontoxic CEOs should appreciate is that it also preserves critical capital for growing the business.

Once you have developed the RFP and submitted it to prospective vendors, you can relax, for about a month. Soon the responses will start filing in and you will need all the discerning energy you can muster. Chapter 5 takes you through the steps of selecting your CSTCM business partner.

Please see the Appendix for a checklist of CSTCM requirements in terms of implementation requirements and project checklist. These summarize all of the narrative in this chapter. It will be helpful to make sure you have incorporated all the necessary aspects of your CSTCM project.

BUILDING YOUR CSTCM PROGRAM

As W. C. Fields said, "There comes a time in the affairs of man when we must take the bull by the tail and face the situation." So, we are now facing it: the cost of CSTCM. For most all of us, asking for money to do the project is the hardest part of the project.

GETTING THE PROJECT FUNDS

You may have submitted your requirements documents to a manager or finance committee to get preapproval for the CSTCM project. Your organization, however, may request that you submit an RFP prior to issuing an authorization to spend money. Regardless of the timing of the approval, one of the tasks in your project plan is to produce a comprehensive budget that takes the entire system cost into consideration. You already know from experience that many hidden costs arise whenever you design a system. In fact, the larger the system, the more hidden costs you will encounter. It is safest to budget for the minimum set of features needed to fulfill the high priority items.

Your budget has to include factors such as any initial purchase of hardware and software upgrades needed for internal servers and user desktops. Even though you haven't selected your vendor or products and services yet, your IT department can help you create a preliminary estimate. Your budget will have to include all of the products and services you will be purchasing from the vendor, including software, data conversion, custom development, training, consulting, and user conferences.

Just because you purchased the software and had training does not mean that it will be an instant and ongoing success. You must also make sure you have ongoing training in your budget to help you long-term. What is it going to cost you yearly to progress with CSTCM? What will future upgrades or new modules to the software cost? What will the software support cost on a yearly basis? What are your ongoing costs of server hardware, operating system, and database upgrades for system hosting? How much will your ASP costs go up on a yearly basis? Can you cap it?

We all know that technology changes frequently. Bill Gates went so far as to tell us that we need information quickly and that innovation in systems causes us "to think, act, react and adapt" at the speed of thought. You need to adapt your systems to be competitive. Having a yearly budget to ensure appropriate technology upgrades will help ensure that your system is current and efficient and bolsters your company's user acceptance and success. Providing for future system budgetary needs gives your program an advantage within your organization.

SELECTING YOUR VENDOR

Once you have received RFP responses from the vendors, look critically at each in terms of how they meet your needs. Use your prioritized requirements document. Narrow your selection to three or four vendors in this first cut. You will want to invite these vendors into your organization to demonstrate their system.

For vendor demonstrations, all CSTCM committee members should be present, in addition to any other system stakeholders. Other company personnel who should help evaluate vendors face-to-face include:

- EHS personnel
- Environmental specialists
- IT personnel
- Purchasing representative
- Materials managers
- Anyone else who will be instrumental in system success

During the vendor demonstration, you should look for:

- Ease of software use
- How the software meets your needs

NONTOXIC TIP

YOU WILL BE RELYING ON MANY PEOPLE TO USE THE CSTCM SYSTEM AND PROMOTE ITS POSITIVE COST-SAVING ATTRIBUTES; INCLUDING THEM IN VENDOR SELECTION IS PARAMOUNT TO RECEIVING INTERNAL PROGRAM SUPPORT.

- Depth and knowledge of the vendor
- Vendor expertise in answering your questions

Ongoing vendor support and partnership will be critical to the success of your CSTCM project. After the demonstrations you should be able to narrow your choices to just a couple of potential vendors.

NONTOXIC TIP

YOU ARE PURCHASING A RELATIONSHIP WITH YOUR VENDOR AS MUCH AS YOU ARE PURCHASING THEIR PRODUCTS.

Product Evaluation Checklist

To help you decide which vendors meet your needs, you will need to evaluate each vendor's products and services on many levels. Below is a list of important considerations for product evaluation:

- *How does the vendor's proposed system meet your requirements?*
  Remember that no vendor software is custom-developed specifically for your organization, so it will not meet every single one of your requirements. A rule of thumb is that if the software meets 75 percent of your requirements it makes more sense to purchase than to try to build a custom software solution.

- *How easy to use is the software?*
  CSTCM touches your entire organization. The software application will be used by many of your employees and must be easy to use, efficient, and intuitive. Take this opportunity to be proactive and think about application training costs and any consulting necessary for a successful implementation.

- *How configurable is the application?*
  Since the application has not been custom written for your organization, consider the application's ability to be configured to your specific needs. For example, if you are planning to implement automated chemical reporting, you need to ensure the application can convert from your unit of measure to the reporting unit of measure. This needs to occur for scientific units of measure as well as ambiguous units such as railcars and palettes. The application

should be able to mimic your inventory model easily. The application should be able to do business the way you do business, not force you to manage your operations the way it wants you to.

- *How easy is it to add on other modules?*
Many times a TCM rollout is done in stages. Secondary labeling and Superfund Amendments and Reauthorization Act (SARA) reporting may not be your first system focus. Perhaps you will want to know how easy it will be to add on modules. These modules may be from a different vendor; therefore a proprietary database instead of an industry-standard database will pose a problem down the road.

- *How easy is to extract data from other systems to use in the new system?*
You may also want to extract data from existing systems for other purposes. Here again, a proprietary system or one where you have to pay the vendor whenever you need data extraction is undesirable. In the future, if you decide not to continue using the software, how easy will it be to get the data? It should be easily accessible outside of the application. You should not need the application to utilize your MSDSs; if you do, it will take a programmer to retrieve these, if it is even possible. More importantly, who owns the data? In the case of converted MSDSs you should always be the data owner; it is the key to your economic improvement compliance.

- *How easy will it be to connect this system to other systems within your organization?*
Is data easily exchanged through an industry-standard mechanism such as XML? Is the backend database proprietary or an industry-standard database? You will want the software to be compatible with industry standards.

- *How easy is it to do custom reporting or to retrieve data from this system to be prepared for importation into other systems?*
Regardless of how many reports the system has, there will always be a need for ones specific to your organization. Can the vendor write custom reports for you that become an integral part of the system? Is the database a standard type that has many report generators so

that you can use your favorite one without having to learn another? Custom report writing capabilities will be important to you.

- *How flexible is the system regarding user-defined fields?*
Regardless of the number of data entry fields the system has, you will always need to define more fields specific to your company. Can the system support user-defined objects that are made up of many fields, including user-defined choice lists? Can the system provide reports in support of your user-defined object? For example, you may want to define an object that depicts the physical attributes of a part such as a battery. The object you define would contain data fields such as those representing weight, height, and method of movement. A truly flexible system will have the ability to grow with the organization, as opposed to becoming obsolete as business needs change.

- *How often does the vendor release new versions?*
You will need to consider the timing of software enhancements for your CSTCM system. If there is an inadvertent bug, how quickly will the vendor supply patches? What constitutes a bug? Answers to these questions will give you insight into the vendor's responsiveness. How does the vendor decide what the new features should be? Will your voice be heard if you request an enhancement that is not just specific to your organization but would also meet the needs of other organizations that use the software? What is the timing of these enhancements? Make sure you are working with a vendor who can and will quickly meet your needs.

- *How proactive is the vendor in ensuring that its software meets the most current regulations?*
What is the depth of the vendor's organization from a training and consulting perspective? Regulatory entities issue frequent changes affecting chemical management; therefore, a good CSTCM solution will be able to respond quickly and effectively to regulatory changes.

- *How good is your vendor's support?*
Like many companies, you may require 24/7 support. If not, you will want support during your normal working hours at the least.

Does the vendor have a toll-free number? Is there also e-mail support? How long on average will you have to wait for answers to your questions? When you call, can you speak with an environmental specialist? Can you talk to a software developer? Is technical support handled by technical personnel, including IT and software-usage experts? A simple test is to call for technical support and see how knowledgeable the person is about their products. Demand that you have access to the people who can help you with ongoing successful solutions. A quality organization will have statistics concerning technical support issues relative to the elapsed time between problem reporting and problem resolution.

NONTOXIC TIP

IF VENDOR SUPPORT ISN'T GOOD IN PRESALE, I CAN PROMISE YOU IT WON'T BE ANY BETTER POST-SALE!

Vendor Attribute Questions Checklist

Evaluating prospective vendors and their products and services is one side of the equation to building a good CSTCM machine; the other is evaluating the vendor as an organization. Below is a list of important considerations for evaluating your prospective vendors. You can probably think of some important criteria of your own to add.

• *What is the vendor's financial strength?*
  During the poor economy of recent years, we have witnessed many small companies in the compliance market close shop and leave their customers with unsupported software and data. Therefore, longevity in the TCM software and services business is important. Ask the vendor for its most current audited financials.

• *What is the vendor's expertise in TCM?*
  The understanding and support of TCM that a vendor shows in each function within its organization is very important. For example, what is the expertise of the developers and consultants? How long have they been with the company? What are their educational backgrounds? What is the installed base of their existing users?

- *What type of consulting is available?*
Does this vendor have environmental, inventory, implementation, IT, and other forms of consulting available? How deep is the talent and service offering at the company? Has your IT group talked with its IT group? What is your IT group's level of comfort with this organization?

- *Who are their salespeople?*
Is your vendor offering you "used-car" salespeople or do they have real-world TCM experience? How long have the salespeople been with the organization? Do they understand your issues? Has their organization been at your disposal during the selection process?

- *What type of training does the vendor offer?*
Does it offer training at your site as well as its own? What other types of information sources does the organization offer? Are there user's conferences? Newsletters? Does the vendor have an informational Web site featuring current issues that are of interest to you?

- *What are the vendor's references like?*
It is important to really check vendor references. Look for references within your business sector as well as other types of businesses. The ability for the vendor's software and services to satisfy many different business sectors is a clue to the flexibility and scope of its products. By talking with the vendor's current customers, you can assess their feelings toward the vendor and its products and services. Do some digging here.

- *Are the products and services you are interested in actually this vendor's core business?*
If the vendor's products and services do not fall within the vendor's core business, they might not be in that business for very long. The vendor may have a great inventory system, but is it oriented toward chemical inventory? Can it handle the real-world nuances of chemical management and reporting?

- *Who is on the vendor's management team?*
What is their expertise and how long have they been with the organization? What are their plans for staying with the organiza-

tion? What is each individual's background, educational experience, and work experience?

• *What is the culture of the organization?*
Because this vendor will be your partner in CSTCM, it is important to know if its culture and cultural values are similar to yours. Make sure that this is an organization that you can entrust with your business.

NONTOXIC TIP

DON'T JUST CALL THE REFERENCES THE VENDOR SUPPLIES. THOSE REFERENCES WILL BE HAND PICKED. LOOK AT THE VENDOR'S WEB SITE TO SEE WHO SOME OF THEIR USERS ARE AND CALL THEM YOURSELF.

Now that you have looked critically at the vendors and their various products and services, it is imperative for your CSTCM team to visit a vendor's site and perform a vendor audit. Truly nontoxic CEOs and their people will want to evaluate each vendor's organizational strength face-to-face.

Vendor Department Audit Checklist

Over the years, I have seen many corporate customers with extremely stringent auditing requirements for their vendors, some due to FDA regulations or, more commonly, their own internal standards. Like these customers, you owe it to yourself, your workers, and the environmental and financial health of your entire organization to audit any compliance software/CSTCM vendor's entire process.

During your on-site visit, carry along a short list of vendor departments to look at closely. This list should include:
• MSDS data conversion
• Chemical data inventory
• Software development
• Technical support
• Customer service

It takes passionate effort for a company to provide the marketplace with world-class data, software, and services. The vendor should have in place clearly stated standard operating procedures that control production and data quality. Its production team should be able to articulate their understanding of the importance of your data. You simply must see and hear what checks and balances are in place to ensure accuracy and on-time delivery of your data. See Figure 14 for a group of audit questions for the data conversion vendor.

By auditing the vendor you will walk away with a good idea of its professional nature and its ability to deliver the top-shelf products and services you deserve.

> **NONTOXIC TIP**
>
> MORE THAN 90 PERCENT OF SUPPORT CALLS SHOULD BE HANDLED SUCCESSFULLY ON THE DAY OF THE CALL.

Other valuable site visits will be to the vendor's current clients, inside and outside of your industry, to see how they are using the vendor's products and services. Again, do a little sleuthing of your own. Call and visit the vendor's clients that you have uncovered, not just the ones the salespeople offer.

If the software meets the majority of the requirements (remember that 75 percent rule) and you like and trust the vendor, then buying the software is a good choice.

If you are considering building your CSTCM software in house, you must consider the expertise of the people who will design, write, enhance, and support the applications. Consider your in-house programmers' ability to have the software ready on your project schedule and their support, training, and new-enhancement capabilities.

When building software in house, you must think about turnover. Turnover invariably means a great loss of knowledge about the system and may leave you without the IT support you need. Buying a software package usually makes more sense because you avoid all of the in-house issues and you can transfer many complex responsibilities to a vendor-partner who has a vested interest in your success. That said, chose a

FIGURE 14.

Specific Questions to Ask Specific People on a Vendor Audit

Audit the vendor's IT group. These are the people who will write the software and possibly host your application. They will provide software enhancements and possibly training.

- What procedures are in place to make sure that the software is bug free?
- What measures ensure timely bug fixes and enhancements?
- What standards are in place in the IT department?
- Are there coding standards?
- Are there SOPs for development and testing?
- Is there a formal system life cycle?
- What are their testing procedures?
- What are their documentation procedures (internal programming documentation and end-user documentation such as help systems)?
- What are their data backup and security procedures?

(If the vendor will be hosting your data, your audit will need to include its internal hardware and network infrastructure or that of their co-location, if applicable.)

Audit the vendor's technical support and customer support group.

- What is the typical time elapsed between first support call and successful issue completion?
- How are support calls tracked?
- How are enhancement requests handled and tracked?

vendor of good reputation who has been in the business for an extended period of time.

NONTOXIC TIP

A VENDOR CAN ALSO PROVIDE CONSULTING AND TRAINING, BRING-ING "REAL-WORLD" EXPERIENCE TO YOUR ORGANIZATION WITH THE DIVERSE KNOWLEDGE OF MANY CLIENTS IN DIFFERENT BUSINESS SECTORS.

DESIGNING YOUR WORK PLAN: GETTING CONTRACTED HELP

So far you have your wish list. CSTCM will require you to get buy-in from many different departments and divisions within your company. In its CSTCM systems development and implementation your company should include employees from:

- Health and safety
- Environmental
- Materials management
- Operations
- Stores
- Site representatives
- Purchasing

Everyone needs to believe that this is not just an expense; CSTCM is a bottom-line value opportunity. So with all these people either living in the house or being close neighbors, it is important to communicate and involve them in the decisions that affect them. Remember that some of these people actually helped build the legacy systems that you may now be enhancing. Ask them for help. Even though you may be going a new direction, the old designer can provide a lot of informa-tion that will help with integration. Another thing to remember, on a holiday weekend, when everything in the house breaks, the old designer may be the only one available to help you, so keeping rela-tionships solid is good insurance against the flood.

YOUR PROJECT PLAN

When you have determined your objectives and have your prioritized requirements document ready, it's time to put together a project plan to ensure that all tasks are considered and all duties are assigned to the appropriate people. A software product such as Microsoft Project or some other project planner may come in handy.

Make sure to consider all project factors so that each task is performed. Review the sample list of tasks in the Appendix. The remainder of this chapter will expand on each of these tasks and provide you with ideas on how to successfully define and implement them.

This project plan should also take into consideration the parts of the project that have a definite timeline. For instance, if part of the project plan is to have a system that facilitates chemical reporting, you will want to take into consideration the next reporting period and whether it is feasible to have a system implemented and working in order to produce needed reports.

If the vendor is having to make some considerable modifications to the product to meet your specific needs, you will want to make sure there is a Service Level Agreement to ensure vendor implementation in the time limit agreed upon. If your timeframe is aggressive, you may have to reduce the features in the first cut of the application or at least be prepared to pay a premium for meeting your desired timeframe.

FOUNDATION: PHYSICAL INVENTORY

Let's say that you decide to do the next step in the process, which is performing a physical inventory. Physical inventories allow you to determine which sites (locations) are using what chemicals. If you are doing an enterprise-wide installation, you will add to the existing electronic database creating site-specific electronic databases that represent products in use. If you are doing a site-by-site installation, physical inventory will be assigning actual site locations to a product only, such as the warehouse the chemical resides in or the shelf in the maintenance department that the oil is on. All MSDSs not assigned to a site as "in use" should be archived or deactivated so as not to confuse system users. This removal of the chemical data will also lower your reporting exposure. Once the database is updated to represent actual chemicals in use, you can start the next stage of the process by focusing on chemical purchasing practices.

CHEMICAL PURCHASING

In order to incorporate CSTCM you want to put limits and controls on the purchasing of chemicals. Chemical purchases come in two types: those that are bought in bulk (usually supply-side management) and those that are bought as small, individual purchases to support maintenance, janitorial services, or small production process. Chemical information from a central store, as well as "P-card" purchases will be useful in highlighting product-specific procurement opportunities. These purchasing processes may show a low percentage of overlap between sites and locations, which may mean uncoordinated purchasing management. It could also mean disparate or unrelated manufacturing processes. A high percentage of product overlap indicates that an opportunity for purchasing leverage exists, which may enable more purchasing discount opportunities.

You may use product overlap to identify the most frequently used products:
- Between sites
- Within business units
- For a corporate-wide view of purchases
- To identify vendor-volume opportunities within chemical groupings
- To negotiate leverage
- To accomplish vendor-side inventorying by region

By automating your chemical management program, your company will receive immediate CSTCM effects, not the least of which is an instant formalization of your material request and approval process. (I promise we will get to material request and approval very soon.)

INVENTORY MANAGEMENT

The next process is inventory management. We can now get into the details of managing inventory with a CSTCM system.

Inventory control is essential to reducing the numbers and volume of hazardous chemicals in your operations. CSTCM, working through your automated MSDSs and linking them with legacy purchasing and inventory systems or leveraging new portable technologies can help you quantify your inventory volumes and values.

It is the nature of modern business that decentralized purchasing practices accumulate loads of particularly hazardous chemicals. You may very well have too many of them in your current operations, which is helping to make your operation toxic. To go back to the example of the "P-card," let's look at the following analogy: A family of four each have their own "P-card" and are responsible for supplying the house with the food they eat. The family will end up with four jars of peanut butter, four bottles of milk, four quarts of chocolate ice cream, and four jars of mayonnaise. By now you probably get the picture. It would be better to pool the money and purchase one of each of the above, save money, and minimize waste.

In CSTCM, we are primarily concerned with software applications that will help you manage chemicals through a true cradle-to-grave process, coming at the task of chemical reduction through the MSDSs.

A good CSTCM system will integrate:

- Material request and approval (to keep the peanut butter purchases in check)
- MSDS management
- Inventory tracking (and perhaps some substitution)
- Ability to report on vendor/supplier optimization
- Regulatory list management
- Company-specific restricted chemical lists
- Chemical reporting

In other words, if we imagine a continuum that represents a chemical in your organization, we start with a formal chemical request and approval process and end with how that chemical is used and/or disposed of. Before CSTCM, MSDSs were simply not being used to their full potential to elicit far-reaching benefits for people, planet, and profits.

MATERIAL REQUESTS, CHEMICAL REVIEW/APPROVAL

Here we are; I had promised we would get here! The material request component of your new CSTCM system will allow users to request approval for a purchase or review an approved chemical list for their locations. You will be able to monitor the types and amounts of your resources. The chemical review and approval process is designed to utilize the information from the requester as the basis for the review and approval process. (In practice, the material requester and reviewer/approver should not be the same person, but your data module ought to be designed to allow maximum flexibility to meet the organizational needs. Here, just like with the use of energy in business, resource conservation is critical.

The five steps below are actionable tasks that relate to the best-practices policies that we established in chapter 4. This process is a plan to chemical reduction; however, remember what our great cowboy philosopher Will Rogers told us: "Plans get you into things, but you've got to work your way out." Material request and approval is your way out, so get to work!

1. Establish approved vendor sources for each chemical product grouping. Too often purchasing motions only consider chemical acquisition costs, and the shelves become jammed with partially used containers from a multitude of vendor sources.

2. Develop procedures for chemical use. To your painting crew an instruction like "use up all the paint in the can" will save untold thousands of dollars in waste disposal and regulatory auditing costs associated with reporting. Combine your "use it up" instruction with "limit the use of aerosol containers" and you have already made a big difference in your maintenance department's impact on waste stream costs. Part of any good, integrated management program is to consider small everyday things as much as the enterprise-wide solutions. And, of course, the more facilities you have, the more the small everyday things are aggregate to big dollars.

3. Establish an automated material request and chemical approval process that considers human and environmental risks before the product is purchased. As discussed, the cost of chemical acquisition

may be only 50 percent to as little as 10 percent of the life-cycle cost of using a particular product at your site.

4. CSTCM produces an immediate toxicity mapping that identifies all chemical products that contain ingredients listed on your elimination list. Attempt to substitute products that are non-hazardous or less toxic. Supply-side chemical management seeks out a limited number of chemical manufactures or vendors and may include significant investment toward the research and development of "green" products. CSTCM assures this work is ongoing and relies on constant vendor communication to ensure that the safest product is used.

5. Review all chemical products against the "use by" dates and dispose of all chemical products that are not in use, unwanted, or obsolete. Some products do not age well and may in fact be degrading on the shelf to form extremely undesirable hazardous waste products through decomposition.

YOU MAY BE USING SOME PART OF THE OLD INFRASTRUCTURE: DATA INTERCHANGE BETWEEN SYSTEMS

In the implementation of any new management system, you will always be faced with exchanging data between systems. Newer database technology, Web applications, and XML (extensible markup language) can simplify this job. In a well-run CSTCM program with smooth data interchange, you can positively affect your daily operations. For instance, if you are purchasing a product in your legacy or ERP system, you may want to determine if that particular product's MSDS is already available. You may also want to know if the amount of chemical product you plan on purchasing breaches any thresholds that will require government reporting. If you had this information at your fingertips and it was near the end of the year, you might not purchase as much to prevent having to report that the chemical was on-site during that year.

XML can be very useful for exchanging data between your legacy purchasing system and new chemical management system. You may also opt for a Web-based system where the product name, manufacturer, product code, or internal part number is passed electronically from legacy systems. Under this scenario, the chemical management system would display a list of matching products and your purchasing personnel could determine if that MSDS is already available and how much product has been purchased or used during any particular time-frame. There may be security issues in exchanging data between the systems, but with the help of your vendor and internal IT group these issues can be easily dealt with.

Above all, the connection between your two systems should be transparent to users. While setting up such systems, I have routinely noticed that users don't need to understand how the systems converse. Users simply need to be able to enter data into one system and have it communicate with the other. Users don't need to be troubled with the details, just delighted with the results.

FINAL NOTES ON BUILDING THE SYSTEM

Implementation is probably the most critical part of the CSTCM process. Since you are the project bandleader, with the challenge of getting everyone in the company to play in harmony and use the system beneficially, it is critical that you put your best foot forward.

Your first job in implementation is to see that the correct hardware and software—on both the server side and client side—is installed and operating correctly. This is usually done on a test server. Give the IT department the opportunity to judge whether this application meets standards of software compatibility with the operating system, database, and other components.

When it is verified that everything works, it can be rolled out to the production environments. Prior to the rollout, make sure all users have been trained correctly. One of the best ways to do this is a "train the trainer" program. In this case the vendor trains people on your staff to train others in your company. The key is to make it easier for people to find their own way; they'll be more successful, more often with this approach.

Finally, you will want to make sure that there is a user's help desk available either on your staff or contracted with the service provider.

There is nothing more frustrating than having a critical piece of software unavailable for use or users misunderstanding how to best use the system. The help desk should provide quick answers to problems and can be the repository for enhancement requests passed on to the vendor.

FINAL INSPECTIONS

Once the software is up and running you need to consistently review how the whole process is working.

CSTCM Review Checklist

Post implementation considerations:
- How is the organization doing according to the original plan?
- Is system success properly documented?
- What management reports are being run from the system?
- Is upper management being given a good understanding of system value?
- Are you listening to user feedback so the system can be made even better?

SHARE YOUR SYSTEM WITH OTHERS

Over the life of your rewarding CSTCM project, you will be the bandleader communicating to all management levels and users the many values that the project brings to your organization. Using all that great data we talked about let everyone know:
- How standardizing chemical requests and approvals has helped.
- How your chemical reduction has increased safety and profits.
- Why more efficient chemical reporting has saved time and money.

As the supplier of positive feedback for management, you need to show the cost savings that have been realized from CSTCM. You should be able to demonstrate this relative to your initial plan. Reinforce that this is not just an expense that allows your company to automate some processes; it's a true source of bottom-line value. Tell your success story. Jim Champy, author of *Reengineering Management and the Arc of Ambition* says, "Storytelling is how human beings relate to each other. Not through business plans. The more senior you are, the more you learn through storytelling."

> ### NONTOXIC TIP
>
> USER CONFERENCES ARE A GREAT TIME TO NETWORK WITH PER-
> SONNEL FROM OTHER COMPANIES THAT UTILIZE THE VENDOR
> SOFTWARE, AND IT IS AN OPPORTUNITY TO WORK WITH THE
> VENDORS AND GET TO KNOW THEIR CONSULTING, SOFTWARE DEVEL-
> OPMENT, AND TRAINING DEPARTMENTS. A CLOSE RELATIONSHIP
> WITH THE VENDOR WILL HELP MAKE SURE YOUR NEEDS ARE HEARD
> AND THAT YOUR PROJECT IS SUCCESSFUL.

UPGRADE AS NECESSARY

To help ensure the continued success of your CSTCM project, implement a system life cycle relative to your project. To do this, you must
constantly monitor the usage of the system and understand any change
in business or user needs. When changes are needed, gather these
requirements and, along with the users, help design new enhancements
or even new modules that can be built to extend the system.

Throughout the software life cycle, there will be new releases from
the vendor or from your internal IT group. Subsequent releases have to
be installed in the same basic way the system was originally implemented. They need to be tested and trained for, and the help desk
needs to be updated on new features before software can be rolled out.
If users are not trained, new features will not be used. Some employees
won't even know that these features exist. Many times I have heard
users complain about how a chemical management system doesn't work
the way they work, when in fact these systems are usually working precisely as planned; someone just dropped the ball and neglected to
properly inform and train the users! Don't shoot yourself in the foot
that way. The ongoing steps for success are a matter of understanding
business needs:

- Work with software designers on your requirements
- Implement your system
- Install software
- Conduct proper training
- Monitor usage
- Evaluate results

- Make necessary changes
- Communicate, communicate, communicate

The process described above must be ongoing. Remember throughout the process of CSTCM you will be "confronted with insurmountable opportunities." My advice is get out the CSTCM ladder and start climbing. The view is better when you can see your entire system.

CHAPTER 6

Maintaining inspiration
and momentum

Business coach Thomas Leonard once said, "Motivation is an external, temporary high that pushes you forward. Inspiration is a sustainable internal glow which pulls you forward."

That's the kind of feeling you want to inspire in people, that internal pull. It's like the undertow you feel at the beach when you're standing barefoot in the ocean as the tide goes out. Let your internal passion for doing the right thing draw you to the greater protection of your people, planet, and profits!

The benefits in human safety and environmental protection that CSTCM offers are strong, emotional drivers for your EHS managers, employees, and specific CSTCM team members. Keeping people safe and the environment healthy is inspirational work; it's not just motivational. Most everyone sees the value of adding to bottom-line profits.

Keeping a strong CSTCM program going is not that different from inspiring employees in any other program you have fostered; it requires a little compassion, great communication and influence skills, and a lot of common sense.

Inspiration at its simplest level fuels needed behavior modification of your managers and employees. But don't forget that you want to modify their behavior internally with a strong appeal to their values and sense of doing the right thing. You do not want to implement and maintain CSTCM or any other program, for that matter, through external pushing.

THE TEAM: ALIGNING INTERESTS

Everyone in the CSTCM program should work together as a team, and that includes your outside vendors. From the beginning you must encourage your people to have a certain degree of autonomy within their departmental group to innovate new and improved chemical management strategies. This will help keep them inspired. Managers

---

NONTOXIC TIP

NO MATTER HOW MANY VENDORS, EMPLOYEES, AND CROSS-DEPART-MENTAL INFLUENCES END UP CONTRIBUTING TO YOUR CSTCM PROGRAM, YOU, THE NONTOXIC CEO, NEED TO BE THE MAIN INSPIRATION.

---

should create and maintain an environment of camaraderie where the employees, as a team, voluntarily pull out the stops to succeed.

As a team, your people develop a level of trust in the good work they do and get to know and understand each other's strengths. Through this the success of the organization will be solidified. The group needs to believe in the company's CSTCM goals. The team members need to be able to express themselves and feel they are an integral part of the overall success of the program.

CASE STUDY: SELECTING PEOPLE FOR THE FUTURE

How do you find the people who will help you foster a long-term vision and create sustainability in your CSTCM program? This case study might shed some light on that question.

One of the best-run organizations in the world is the Salvation Army. The Salvation Army people ask for a lifetime commitment to the organization. Its technique is to put people in training positions for nearly two years before cutting them loose in their own territory. The officers are then allowed to run programs that are necessary, given their particular environment. Inner-city programs are different than rural programs. Some Salvation Army outposts run drug rehab centers; others have day care operations. The Salvation Army captains are trained in the values of the organization, put into training situations that allow them to learn from the top commanders, and then they are empowered.

While a nontoxic CEO cannot expect the commitment of employees for life to a CSTCM program, people can be inspired and trained to maintain momentum with a commitment to the values in the organization. This is done through their ability to align their personal values with the values of the organization.

> ### NONTOXIC TIP
>
> TO ENSURE THE SUSTAINABILITY OF YOUR CSTCM PROGRAM, INSPIRE AND TRAIN PEOPLE WHO WANT TO BE A PART OF THE WORTHWHILE BENEFITS OF PROTECTING PEOPLE, THE PLANET, AND COMPANY PROFITABILITY.

Finally, don't forget the bandleader advice from chapter 1. Your goal as the nontoxic CEO is to inspire boundless enthusiasm and encourage your staff to have a winning attitude. Inspiration moves people. The power of doing positive work that makes a major contribution to human safety and environmental health can supercharge your productivity.

> ### NONTOXIC TIP
>
> THROUGHOUT YOUR CSTCM PROGRAM, MAINTAIN A TRIPLE FOCUS WHERE EVERYONE'S AIMS ARE COORDINATED: ALIGN THE INTERESTS OF THE INDIVIDUAL, THE TEAM, AND THE ORGANIZATION WITH THE SAME GOAL IN MIND.

MOMENTUM: THE ART OF ROLLING THE BALL

Anyone who has watched sports understands the law of momentum. When you have it, you have the edge. When the game starts or the race begins, everything moves toward that final buzzer or the finish line. While momentum is important to winning a game with a finite time limit or finish in sight, it is just as important in an ongoing game or a race.

In dealing with your ongoing CSTCM and any other EHS management program, it may be easier to think about your goals as a series of games over several seasons. Theoretically, with each game, players are starting to know the plays, know each other, and increase their performance capacity. There are times for each game to end and for the team to sit back, analyze the results, and get ready for the next game.

The strategies in this book assume that you are the bandleader or, to use our recent sports metaphor, the coach. If you are not the actual company CEO but have been given the responsibility of being the bandleader/coach of your own turf within the EHS organization, then you are a decision maker and a resource locator. Regardless of your actual job title, you will run up against the issue of momentum and motivation.

YOU MUST STAY FOCUSED

Those of us who have spent time educating ourselves (or our children) understand the "sophomore slump." There is a time in the sophomore year where there is little energy to go on, not much light at the end of the tunnel, and zero hindsight. Professional projects take on a similar life cycle. It is during this period that you have to brace yourself. It is when you must rely on previous professional and personal experience to back up what you know to be truth for your project. This is the time to ensure that your people do not give up or drop out.

Your CSTCM coworkers must be people who share your vision for the company's chemical management program. Think of the team that works at 3M. Can you imagine a company with a commitment to environmental management so strong and sustained that has consistently improved its performance annually for more than 28 years now, without a break, yielding billions of dollars? That means that no matter how many dips in the economy, or personnel turnover, for more than a quarter-century the program keeps getting more productive. It really is possible for a company of any size to maintain momentum if everyone pulls together under strong leaders with a unified vision.

BE PREPARED FOR CHANGE

A second reality is the ephemeral nature of business: things change. Robert Shakleton, the great Antarctic Explorer, made an art form of the technique of harnessing change as a momentum builder. One of Shakleton's expedition crew members explained, "Well-settled plans would suddenly be changed with little warning and a new set made. This was apt to be a little bewildering, but it generally turned out to be for the good. Adaptability was one of his strong points. With him it was never a wavering between two ideas. It was a conviction that the second one was a better one and so we acted accordingly."

Change occurs in many ways. Be innovative and let business units or divisions try some of the ideas they have been begging to execute. Go out on a limb and take a risk. Never be afraid to create some chaos, just as long as it's well-reasoned, positive results-producing chaos. There will be changes periodically on an internal basis (within your company's direction) and an external one (the state of the market or the economy). When the change happens, challenge yourself and others to find a new approach to the program that is inclusive of the latest direction of the company, the marketplace, your competitors, your customers, and/or the economy. Though your methods may change, never lose sight of your goal: protecting your people, planet, and profits. You will still want to manage your chemicals and your company responsibly, regardless of changes.

NONTOXIC TIP

IF YOUR CSTCM PROGRAM IS BUILT ON A PHILOSOPHY THAT POSITIVE CHANGE IS NOT ONLY GOOD BUT REQUIRED, THE ORGANIZATION WILL OUTLIVE THE IMPLEMENTATION PROCESS AND ENCOURAGE EACH PLAYER TO WORK TOWARD SUSTAINING THE PROGRAM.

MAKING GOOD BETTER

A third aspect of proper program management is to strive for continuous improvement. That's not '90s management book rhetoric; it is a reality of any living system. You must incorporate learning and growing into your CSTCM program. One way to ensure increases in excellence and continuously improved performance is through your process for information gathering and sharing. Be ever curious about ways to do things better and encourage your team members to do the same.

Make sure that CSTCM systems that don't contribute to your results measurement phase get scrapped or modified. Create a structure that constantly reviews the needs and opportunities to change. Your processes must be able to do the same thing. Ask yourself if the needs for your people, planet, and profits are the same today as they were when your system was established. As management guru Peter Drucker says, "You will never make perfect decisions, just imperfect decisions that make a real difference."

The final part of maintaining knowledge-growth in the organization is to make sure that you are able to adapt when your system is forced to change due to new technologies. People may need to be moved into different areas and new blood injected into the organization to adapt to new technologies, but it will be worth the effort.

YOU WON'T KNOW EVERYTHING

As you develop your program, be careful to teach your people that there is value in the process of learning. As EHS specialists and protectors of people and the planet, we are always learning more. Also be aware that there is one thing that makes your not knowing critical and serves to make people anxious: not knowing everything in the high-stakes arena of toxic chemicals can risk someone's life. Be aware that each situation that you deal with affects a bigger part of the system.

NONTOXIC TIP

DO NOT UNDERESTIMATE THE PR HEALING EFFECT, BOTH INTERNAL AND EXTERNAL.

SUSTAIN VISIBILITY

Another eventuality to prepare for is the day when the very people who asked you to build a process for better chemical management forget why you are doing the program. To prevent such an occurrence, don't stop selling the process, your results, and the opportunity to enhance the process.

Maintaining momentum requires sustaining visibility. In hard economic times, this means trumpeting the ROI of better chemical management. You will partly maintain your CSTCM momentum through measurement and assessment, but success does not come from that alone. You must keep your positive measurements—and what is being measured—visible, vital, and vibrant.

DON'T LEAVE, BUT PLAN FOR YOUR DEPARTURE

One healthy way to make your CSTCM program bulletproof for the long haul is to periodically ask yourself, "What if I were not here to lead this?" Of course, you do not want to leave your job as the program bandleader until you can honestly answer the above question with the affirmation that a process and living model exists for protecting your company's people, planet, and profits. There are many capable people in your organization. It must be a part of your plan that without your leadership, the program can still continue. With CSTCM you are creating a workable system and more; you are creating a sustainable legacy. It is the people you leave behind who will do the job ahead.

THE SYSTEM IS THE GOAL

Throughout your mission in building a system of better chemical management, you will find success by educating others, communicating, working hard, evaluating, re-evaluating, measuring, and adapting to change, and helping others do the same.

Ultimately, you will reach your finish line many times. Each quarter and each year that you can evaluate your results, you will realize that you really have made your workers safer, reduced your inventory (and possibly emissions and disposal) of hazardous chemicals, and that your bottom line looks better because of CSTCM.

As you build and maintain momentum, allow yourself enough of a break to understand that though you may stumble occasionally on your way to your goal, safer, cleaner, more profitable chemical management is a moving finish line worth striving toward.

APPENDIX

YOUR CSTCM PROJECT CHECKLIST

❏ All organizational stakeholders sign off on the requirements and priorities.

❏ If you are not choosing an ASP solution, develop a comprehensive budget that takes into consideration items paid by corporate and the items passed on to the sites.

❏ Develop a list of all computing resources you will need from the IT department in terms of hardware, software, networking, etc. Make sure you take into consideration desktop costs for each user, as well as server hardware and software.

❏ Research vendors who can provide the CSTCM solution you have designed.

❏ Write the RFP that will be sent to each vendor; include a timeline of when you expect these RFPs back.

❏ Set a date for evaluating the RFPs that have been returned from vendors.

❏ Determine a final vendor selection date on which the committee selects three or four vendors who can meet the requirements.

❏ Set a date to invite these vendors to your organization for a demonstration of their products and services. Make sure that all committee members are present.

❏ Allow time for visiting the vendors and seeing first-hand the quality of their products and services and the culture of the organization.

❏ Set aside time to visit some of the vendor's customers within your industry and, if possible, other industries as well.

❏ Set a date to select and notify the final vendor.

❏ Create a task for purchasing and contracts to finish negotiating the deal.

❏ Develop tasks for implementation and testing of the CSTCM solution.

❏ Design the interfaces to existing legacy data, if necessary. For instance, an MSDS system can be tied to purchasing to determine if a sheet exists at the time a product is being ordered.

❏ Develop a timeline for having the vendor "train the trainer" and train users. This also assists in setting up a help desk if necessary.

❏ Finally, roll out the solution and follow up to evaluate how it is working.

WHAT TO LOOK AT IN CSTCM IMPLEMENTATION

- Your current system (ERP or otherwise)
- Graphic depiction of your existing system
- Identifying CSTCM players at your organization
- Designing a new system
- Prioritizing your requirements
- Planning your project
- Budgeting
- System design and technology
- Existing data preservation
- Existing data interchange
- Chemical data and services
- ASPs vs. traditional software purchases
- The entire vendor evaluation and selection process
- Making vs. buying a system
- System implementation
- System review
- Ongoing steps for success
- Answering naysayers

SAMPLE MATERIAL SAFETY DATA SHEET (MSDS)

```
MATERIAL SAFETY DATA SHEET

MSDS: 10298

REVISION #: 2

REVISION DATE: 5/16/2002

24-HOUR EMERGENCY TELEPHONE NUMBERS:
HEALTH: EMERGENCY INFORMATION CENTER
TRANSPORTATION:

EMERGENCY INFORMATION CENTERS ARE LOCATED IN THE U.S.A. INTERNATIONAL
COLLECT CALLS ACCEPTED.


------SECTION 1 PRODUCT AND COMPANY IDENTIFICATION ------

ANTI-FREEZE COOLANT

PRODUCT NUMBER(S): CPS222353


------SECTION 2 COMPOSITION/INFORMATION ON INGREDIENTS ------

COMPONENTS               CAS NUMBER      AMOUNT

ETHYLENE GLYCOL          107-21-1        90-96.99 %WEIGHT

DIETHYLENE GLYCOL        111-46-6        1-4.99 %WEIGHT

WATER                    7732-18-5       1-4.99 %WEIGHT

DIPOTASSIUM PHOSPHATE     7758-11-4       1-2.99 %WEIGHT


------SECTION 3 HAZARDS IDENTIFICATION ------

EMERGENCY OVERVIEW:

FLUORESCENT GREEN LIQUID. MILD ODOR.

-HARMFUL OR FATAL IF SWALLOWED
-CAUSES EYE IRRITATION
-POSSIBLE BIRTH DEFECT HAZARD - CONTAINS MATERIAL THAT MAY CAUSE BIRTH
DEFECTS BASED ON ANIMAL DATA
-MAY CAUSE DAMAGE TO:
-KIDNEY

IMMEDIATE HEALTH EFFECTS:

EYE:
CONTACT WITH THE EYES CAUSES IRRITATION. SYMPTOMS MAY INCLUDE PAIN, TEARING,
REDDENING, SWELLING AND IMPAIRED VISION.

SKIN:
CONTACT WITH THE SKIN IS NOT EXPECTED TO CAUSE PROLONGED OR SIGNIFICANT
```

IRRITATION. NOT EXPECTED TO BE HARMFUL TO INTERNAL ORGANS IF ABSORBED THROUGH THE SKIN.

INGESTION: TOXIC; MAY BE HARMFUL OR FATAL IF SWALLOWED.

INHALATION:
THE VAPOR OR FUMES FROM THIS MATERIAL MAY CAUSE RESPIRATORY IRRITATION. SYMPTOMS OF RESPIRATORY IRRITATION MAY INCLUDE COUGHING AND DIFFICULTY BREATHING.

DELAYED OR OTHER HEALTH EFFECTS:
CONTAINS MATERIAL THAT MAY BE HARMFUL TO THE DEVELOPING FETUS BASED ON ANIMAL DATA.

TARGET ORGANS:
CONTAINS MATERIAL THAT MAY CAUSE DAMAGE TO THE FOLLOWING ORGAN(S) FOLLOWING REPEATED INGESTION BASED ON ANIMAL DATA: KIDNEY

SEE SECTION 11 FOR ADDITIONAL INFORMATION. RISK DEPENDS ON DURATION AND LEVEL OF EXPOSURE.

------SECTION 4 FIRST AID MEASURES ------

EYE:
FLUSH EYES WITH WATER IMMEDIATELY WHILE HOLDING THE EYELIDS OPEN. REMOVE CONTACT LENSES, IF WORN, AFTER INITIAL FLUSHING, AND CONTINUE FLUSHING FOR AT LEAST 15 MINUTES. GET MEDICAL ATTENTION IF IRRITATION PERSISTS.

SKIN:
TO REMOVE THE MATERIAL FROM SKIN, USE SOAP AND WATER. DISCARD CONTAMINATED CLOTHING AND SHOES OR THOROUGHLY CLEAN BEFORE REUSE.

INGESTION:
IF SWALLOWED, GET IMMEDIATE MEDICAL ATTENTION. DO NOT INDUCE VOMITING. NEVER GIVE ANYTHING BY MOUTH TO AN UNCONSCIOUS PERSON.

INHALATION:
MOVE THE EXPOSED PERSON TO FRESH AIR. IF NOT BREATHING, GIVE ARTIFICIAL RESPIRATION. IF BREATHING IS DIFFICULT, GIVE OXYGEN. GET MEDICAL ATTENTION IF BREATHING DIFFICULTIES CONTINUE.

------SECTION 5 FIRE FIGHTING MEASURES ------

FIRE CLASSIFICATION:
OSHA CLASSIFICATION (29 CFR 1910.1200):
NOT CLASSIFIED BY OSHA AS FLAMMABLE OR COMBUSTIBLE.

NFPA RATINGS:
HEALTH: 2
FLAMMABILITY: 1
REACTIVITY: 0

FLAMMABLE PROPERTIES:

FLASHPOINT: (PENSKY-MARTENS CLOSED CUP) 260 DEG. F (127 DEG. C)

AUTOIGNITION: NDA

FLAMMABILITY (EXPLOSIVE) LIMITS (% BY VOLUME IN AIR):
LOWER: 3.2
UPPER:

EXTINGUISHING MEDIA: DRY CHEMICAL, CO2, AFFF FOAM OR ALCOHOL RESISTANT FOAM.

PROTECTION OF FIRE FIGHTERS:

FIRE FIGHTING INSTRUCTIONS:
THIS MATERIAL WILL BURN ALTHOUGH IT IS NOT EASILY IGNITED. FOR FIRES
INVOLVING THIS MATERIAL, DO NOT ENTER ANY ENCLOSED OR CONFINED FIRE SPACE
WITHOUT PROPER PROTECTIVE EQUIPMENT, INCLUDING SELF-CONTAINED BREATHING
APPARATUS.

COMBUSTION PRODUCTS:
HIGHLY DEPENDENT ON COMBUSTION CONDITIONS. A COMPLEX MIXTURE OF AIRBORNE
SOLIDS, LIQUIDS, AND GASES INCLUDING CARBON MONOXIDE, CARBON DIOXIDE, AND
UNIDENTIFIED ORGANIC COMPOUNDS WILL BE EVOLVED WHEN THIS MATERIAL UNDERGOES
COMBUSTION. COMBUSTION MAY FORM OXIDES OF: PHOSPHORUS, POTASSIUM.

------SECTION 6 ACCIDENTAL RELEASE MEASURES ------

PROTECTIVE MEASURES:
ELIMINATE ALL SOURCES OF IGNITION IN VICINITY OF SPILLED MATERIAL.

SPILL MANAGEMENT:
STOP THE SOURCE OF THE RELEASE IF YOU CAN DO IT WITHOUT RISK. CONTAIN
RELEASE TO PREVENT FURTHER CONTAMINATION OF SOIL, SURFACE WATER OR
GROUNDWATER. CLEAN UP SPILL AS SOON AS POSSIBLE, OBSERVING PRECAUTIONS IN
EXPOSURE CONTROLS/PERSONAL PROTECTION. USE APPROPRIATE TECHNIQUES SUCH AS
APPLYING NON-COMBUSTIBLE ABSORBENT MATERIALS OR PUMPING. WHERE FEASIBLE AND
APPROPRIATE, REMOVE CONTAMINATED SOIL. PLACE CONTAMINATED MATERIALS IN
DISPOSABLE CONTAINERS AND DISPOSE OF IN A MANNER CONSISTENT WITH APPLICABLE
REGULATIONS.

REPORTING:
REPORT SPILLS TO LOCAL AUTHORITIES AND/OR THE U.S. COAST GUARD'S NATIONAL
RESPONSE CENTER AT (800) 424-8802 AS APPROPRIATE OR REQUIRED.

------SECTION 7 HANDLING AND STORAGE ------

PRECAUTIONARY MEASURES:
DO NOT GET IN EYES. WASH THOROUGHLY AFTER HANDLING. DO NOT BREATHE VAPOR OR
FUMES.

GENERAL HANDLING INFORMATION:
DO NOT TASTE OR SWALLOW ANTIFREEZE OR SOLUTION. KEEP OUT OF THE REACH OF
CHILDREN AND ANIMALS.

STATIC HAZARD:
ELECTROSTATIC CHARGE MAY ACCUMULATE AND CREATE A HAZARDOUS CONDITION WHEN
HANDLING THIS MATERIAL. TO MINIMIZE THIS HAZARD, BONDING AND GROUNDING MAY

BE NECESSARY BUT MAY NOT, BY THEMSELVES, BE SUFFICIENT. REVIEW ALL OPERATIONS WHICH HAVE THE POTENTIAL OF GENERATING AN ACCUMULATION OF ELECTROSTATIC CHARGE AND/OR A FLAMMABLE ATMOSPHERE (INCLUDING TANK AND CONTAINER FILLING, SPLASH FILLING, TANK CLEANING, SAMPLING, GAUGING, SWITCH LOADING, FILTERING, MIXING, AGITATION, AND VACUUM TRUCK OPERATIONS) AND USE APPROPRIATE MITIGATING PROCEDURES. FOR MORE INFORMATION, REFER TO OSHA STANDARD 29 CFR 1910.106, 'FLAMMABLE AND COMBUSTIBLE LIQUIDS', NATIONAL FIRE PROTECTION ASSOCIATION (NFPA 77, 'RECOMMENDED PRACTICE ON STATIC ELECTRICITY', AND/OR THE AMERICAN PETROLEUM INSTITUTE (API) RECOMMENDED PRACTICE 2003, 'PROTECTION AGAINST IGNITIONS ARISING OUT OF STATIC, LIGHTNING, AND STRAY CURRENTS'.

GENERAL STORAGE INFORMATION: DO NOT STORE IN OPEN OR UNLABELED CONTAINERS.

CONTAINER WARNINGS:
CONTAINER IS NOT DESIGNED TO CONTAIN PRESSURE. DO NOT USE PRESSURE TO EMPTY CONTAINER OR IT MAY RUPTURE WITH EXPLOSIVE FORCE. EMPTY CONTAINERS RETAIN PRODUCT RESIDUE (SOLID, LIQUID, AND/OR VAPOR) AND CAN BE DANGEROUS. DO NOT PRESSURIZE, CUT, WELD, BRAZE, SOLDER, DRILL, GRIND, OR EXPOSE SUCH CONTAINERS TO HEAT, FLAME, SPARKS, STATIC ELECTRICITY, OR OTHER SOURCES OF IGNITION. THEY MAY EXPLODE AND CAUSE INJURY OR DEATH. EMPTY CONTAINERS SHOULD BE COMPLETELY DRAINED, PROPERLY CLOSED, AND PROMPTLY RETURNED TO A DRUM RECONDITIONER OR DISPOSED OF PROPERLY.

------SECTION 8 EXPOSURE CONTROLS/PERSONAL PROTECTION ------

GENERAL CONSIDERATIONS:
CONSIDER THE POTENTIAL HAZARDS OF THIS MATERIAL (SEE SECTION 3), APPLICABLE EXPOSURE LIMITS, JOB ACTIVITIES, AND OTHER SUBSTANCES IN THE WORK PLACE WHEN DESIGNING ENGINEERING CONTROLS AND SELECTING PERSONAL PROTECTIVE EQUIPMENT. IF ENGINEERING CONTROLS OR WORK PRACTICES ARE NOT ADEQUATE TO PREVENT EXPOSURE TO HARMFUL LEVELS OF THIS MATERIAL, THE PERSONAL PROTECTIVE EQUIPMENT LISTED BELOW IS RECOMMENDED. THE USER SHOULD READ AND UNDERSTAND ALL INSTRUCTIONS AND LIMITATIONS SUPPLIED WITH THE EQUIPMENT SINCE PROTECTION IS USUALLY PROVIDED FOR A LIMITED TIME OR UNDER CERTAIN CIRCUMSTANCES.

ENGINEERING CONTROLS:
USE PROCESS ENCLOSURES, LOCAL EXHAUST VENTILATION, OR OTHER ENGINEERING CONTROLS TO CONTROL AIRBORNE LEVELS BELOW THE RECOMMENDED EXPOSURE LIMITS.

PERSONAL PROTECTIVE EQUIPMENT:

EYE/FACE PROTECTION:
WEAR EYE PROTECTION SUCH AS SAFETY GLASSES, CHEMICAL GOGGLES, OR FACESHIELDS IF ENGINEERING CONTROLS OR WORK PRACTICES ARE NOT ADEQUATE TO PREVENT EYE CONTACT.

SKIN PROTECTION:
NO SPECIAL PROTECTIVE CLOTHING IS NORMALLY REQUIRED. WHERE SPLASHING IS POSSIBLE, SELECT PROTECTIVE CLOTHING DEPENDING ON OPERATIONS CONDUCTED, PHYSICAL REQUIREMENTS AND OTHER SUBSTANCES. SUGGESTED MATERIALS FOR PROTECTIVE GLOVES INCLUDE: NATURAL RUBBER, NEOPRENE, NITRILE RUBBER, POLYVINYL CHLORIDE (PVC OR VINYL).

RESPIRATORY PROTECTION:

DETERMINE IF AIRBORNE CONCENTRATIONS ARE BELOW THE RECOMMENDED EXPOSURE
LIMITS. IF NOT, WEAR AN APPROVED RESPIRATOR THAT PROVIDES ADEQUATE
PROTECTION FROM MEASURED CONCENTRATIONS OF THIS MATERIAL, SUCH AS:
AIR-PURIFYING RESPIRATOR FOR ORGANIC VAPORS, DUSTS AND MISTS.
USE A POSITIVE PRESSURE AIR-SUPPLYING RESPIRATOR IN CIRCUMSTANCES WHERE
AIR-PURIFYING RESPIRATORS MAY NOT PROVIDE ADEQUATE PROTECTION.

OCCUPATIONAL EXPOSURE LIMITS:

COMPONENT	LIMIT	TWA	STEL	CEILING	NOTATION
ETHYLENE GLYCOL	ACGIH_TLV			100 MG/M3	
ETHYLENE GLYCOL	OSHA_PEL			125 MG/M3	

------SECTION 9 PHYSICAL AND CHEMICAL PROPERTIES ------

APPEARANCE AND ODOR: FLUORESCENT GREEN LIQUID. MILD ODOR.

pH: 10.2-11

VAPOR PRESSURE: <0.1 MM HG @ 20 DEG. C

VAPOR DENSITY (AIR = 1): 2.1 (TYPICAL)

BOILING POINT: 226 DEG. F (109 C)

SOLUBILITY: MISCIBLE

FREEZING POINT: -34 DEG. F (-37 C)

SPECIFIC GRAVITY: 1.13 @ 15.6 DEG. C/15.6 DEG. C

VISCOSITY: 17.3 CP @ 25 DEG. C (TYPICAL)

------SECTION 10 STABILITY AND REACTIVITY ------

CHEMICAL STABILITY:
THIS MATERIAL IS CONSIDERED STABLE UNDER NORMAL AMBIENT AND ANTICIPATED
STORAGE AND HANDLING CONDITIONS OF TEMPERATURE AND PRESSURE.

INCOMPATIBILITY WITH OTHER MATERIALS:
MAY REACT WITH STRONG OXIDIZING AGENTS, SUCH AS CHLORATES, NITRATES,
PEROXIDES, ETC.

HAZARDOUS DECOMPOSITION PRODUCTS:
KETONES (ELEVATED TEMPERATURES), ALDEHYDES (ELEVATED TEMPERATURES)

HAZARDOUS POLYMERIZATION: HAZARDOUS POLYMERIZATION WILL NOT OCCUR.

------SECTION 11 TOXICOLOGICAL INFORMATION ------

IMMEDIATE HEALTH EFFECTS:

EYE IRRITATION:
THE EYE IRRITATION HAZARD IS BASED ON EVALUATION OF DATA FOR SIMILAR
MATERIALS OR PRODUCT COMPONENTS.

SKIN IRRITATION:
THE SKIN IRRITATION HAZARD IS BASED ON EVALUATION OF DATA FOR SIMILAR
MATERIALS OR PRODUCT COMPONENTS.

SKIN SENSITIZATION: NO PRODUCT TOXICOLOGY DATA AVAILABLE.

ACUTE DERMAL TOXICITY:
THE ACUTE DERMAL TOXICITY HAZARD IS BASED ON EVALUATION OF DATA FOR SIMILAR
MATERIALS OR PRODUCT COMPONENTS.

ACUTE ORAL TOXICITY:
THE ACUTE ORAL TOXICITY HAZARD IS BASED ON EVALUATION OF DATA FOR SIMILAR
MATERIALS OR PRODUCT COMPONENTS.

ACUTE INHALATION TOXICITY:
THE ACUTE INHALATION TOXICITY HAZARD IS BASED ON EVALUATION OF DATA FOR
SIMILAR MATERIALS OR PRODUCT COMPONENTS.

ADDITIONAL TOXICOLOGY INFORMATION:
THIS PRODUCT CONTAINS ETHYLENE GLYCOL (EG). THE TOXICITY OF EG VIA
INHALATION OR SKIN CONTACT IS EXPECTED TO BE SLIGHT AT ROOM TEMPERATURE. THE
ESTIMATED ORAL LETHAL DOSE IS ABOUT 100 CC (3.3 OZ.) FOR AN ADULT HUMAN.
ETHYLENE GLYCOL IS OXIDIZED TO OXALIC ACID WHICH RESULTS IN THE DEPOSITION
OF CALCIUM OXALATE CRYSTALS MAINLY IN THE BRAIN AND KIDNEYS. EARLY SIGNS AND
SYMPTOMS OF EG POISONING MAY RESEMBLE THOSE OF ALCOHOL INTOXICATION. LATER,
THE VICTIM MAY EXPERIENCE NAUSEA, VOMITING, WEAKNESS, ABDOMINAL AND MUSCLE
PAIN, DIFFICULTY IN BREATHING AND DECREASED URINE OUTPUT. WHEN EG WAS HEATED
ABOVE THE BOILING POINT OF WATER, VAPORS FORMED WHICH REPORTEDLY CAUSED
UNCONSCIOUSNESS, INCREASED LYMPHOCYTE COUNT, AND A RAPID, JERKY MOVEMENT OF
THE EYES IN PERSONS CHRONICALLY EXPOSED. WHEN EG WAS ADMINISTERED ORALLY TO
PREGNANT RATS AND MICE, THERE WAS AN INCREASE IN FETAL DEATHS AND BIRTH
DEFECTS. SOME OF THESE EFFECTS OCCURRED AT DOSES THAT HAD NO TOXIC EFFECTS
ON THE MOTHERS. WE ARE NOT AWARE OF ANY REPORTS THAT EG CAUSES REPRODUCTIVE
TOXICITY IN HUMAN BEINGS.

THIS PRODUCT CONTAINS DIETHYLENE GLYCOL (DEG.) THE ESTIMATED ORAL LETHAL
DOSE IS ABOUT 50 CC (1.6 OZ) FOR AN ADULT HUMAN.
DEG HAS CAUSED THE FOLLOWING EFFECTS IN LABORATORY ANIMALS: LIVER
ABNORMALITIES, KIDNEY DAMAGE AND BLOOD ABNORMALITIES.
IT HAS BEEN SUGGESTED AS A CAUSE OF THE FOLLOWING EFFECTS IN HUMANS: LIVER
ABNORMALITIES, KIDNEY DAMAGE, LUNG DAMAGE AND CENTRAL NERVOUS SYSTEM DAMAGE.

------SECTION 12 ECOLOGICAL INFORMATION ------

ECOTOXICITY:
THE TOXICITY OF THIS MATERIAL TO AQUATIC ORGANISMS HAS NOT BEEN EVALUATED.
CONSEQUENTLY, THIS MATERIAL SHOULD BE KEPT OUT OF SEWAGE AND DRAINAGE
SYSTEMS AND ALL BODIES OF WATER.

ENVIRONMENTAL FATE: THIS MATERIAL IS EXPECTED TO BE READILY BIODEGRADABLE.

Sample MSDS, Page 6 of 9

------SECTION 13 DISPOSAL CONSIDERATIONS ------

USE MATERIAL FOR ITS INTENDED PURPOSE OR RECYCLE IF POSSIBLE. THIS MATERIAL,
IF IT MUST BE DISCARDED, MAY MEET THE CRITERIA OF A HAZARDOUS WASTE AS
DEFINED BY US EPA UNDER RCRA (40 CFR 261) OR OTHER STATE AND LOCAL
REGULATIONS. MEASUREMENT OF CERTAIN PHYSICAL PROPERTIES AND ANALYSIS FOR
REGULATED COMPONENTS MAY BE NECESSARY TO MAKE A CORRECT DETERMINATION. IF
THIS MATERIAL IS CLASSIFIED AS A HAZARDOUS WASTE, FEDERAL LAW REQUIRES
DISPOSAL AT A LICENSED HAZARDOUS WASTE DISPOSAL FACILITY.

------SECTION 14 TRANSPORT INFORMATION ------

THE DESCRIPTION SHOWN MAY NOT APPLY TO ALL SHIPPING SITUATIONS. CONSULT
49CFR, OR APPROPRIATE DANGEROUS GOODS REGULATIONS, FOR ADDITIONAL
DESCRIPTION REQUIREMENTS (E.G., TECHNICAL NAME) AND MODE-SPECIFIC OR
QUANTITY-SPECIFIC SHIPPING REQUIREMENTS.

DOT SHIPPING NAME:
NOT REGULATED AS A HAZARDOUS MATERIAL FOR TRANSPORTATION UNDER 49 CFR

DOT HAZARD CLASS: NOT APPLICABLE

DOT IDENTIFICATION NUMBER: NOT APPLICABLE

DOT PACKING GROUP: NOT APPLICABLE

------SECTION 15 REGULATORY INFORMATION ------

SARA 311/312 CATEGORIES:
1. IMMEDIATE (ACUTE) HEALTH EFFECTS: YES
2. DELAYED (CHRONIC) HEALTH EFFECTS: YES
3. FIRE HAZARD: NO
4. SUDDEN RELEASE OF PRESSURE HAZARD: NO
5. REACTIVITY HAZARD: NO

REGULATORY LISTS SEARCHED:
4-I1=IARC GROUP 1
4-I2A=IARC GROUP 2A
4-I2B=IARC GROUP 2B
05=NTP CARCINOGEN
06=OSHA CARCINOGEN
09=TSCA 12(B)
10=TSCA SECTION 4
11=TSCA SECTION 8(A) CAIR
12=TSCA SECTION 8(A) PAIR
13=TSCA SECTION 8(D)
15=SARA SECTION 313
16=CA PROPOSITION 65
17=MA RTK
18=NJ RTK
19=DOT MARINE POLLUTANT
20=PA RTK
21=TSCA SECTION 5(A)
25=CAA SECTION 112 HAPS
26=CWA SECTION 311

```
28=CWA SECTION 307
30=RCRA WASTE P-LIST
31=RCRA WASTE U-LIST
32=RCRA APPENDIX VIII
```

THE FOLLOWING COMPONENTS OF THIS MATERIAL ARE FOUND ON THE REGULATORY LISTS INDICATED.

DIETHYLENE GLYCOL: 25

ETHYLENE GLYCOL: 15, 17, 18, 20, 25

CERCLA REPORTABLE QUANTITIES (RQ)/SARA 302 THRESHOLD PLANNING QUANTITIES (TPQ):

COMPONENT	COMPONENT RQ	COMPONENT TPQ	PRODUCT RQ
ETHYLENE GLYCOL	5000 LBS	NONE	5269 LBS

CHEMICAL INVENTORIES:

AUSTRALIA:
ALL THE COMPONENTS OF THIS MATERIAL ARE LISTED ON THE AUSTRALIAN INVENTORY OF CHEMICAL SUBSTANCES (AICS).

CANADA:
ALL THE COMPONENTS OF THIS MATERIAL ARE ON THE CANADIAN DOMESTIC SUBSTANCES LIST (DSL).

PEOPLE'S REPUBLIC OF CHINA:
ALL THE COMPONENTS OF THIS PRODUCT ARE LISTED ON THE DRAFT INVENTORY OF EXISTING CHEMICAL SUBSTANCES IN CHINA.

EUROPEAN UNION:
ALL THE COMPONENTS OF THIS MATERIAL ARE IN COMPLIANCE WITH THE EU SEVENTH AMENDMENT DIRECTIVE 92/32/EEC.

KOREA:
ALL THE COMPONENTS OF THIS PRODUCT ARE ON THE EXISTING CHEMICALS LIST (ECL) IN KOREA.

PHILIPPINES:
ALL THE COMPONENTS OF THIS PRODUCT ARE LISTED ON THE PHILLIPINE INVENTORY OF CHEMICALS AND CHEMICAL SUBSTANCES (PICCS).

UNITED STATES:
ALL OF THE COMPONENTS OF THIS MATERIAL ARE ON THE TOXIC SUBSTANCES CONTROL ACT (TSCA) CHEMICAL INVENTORY.

NEW JERSEY RTK CLASSIFICATION: REFER TO COMPONENTS LISTED IN SECTION 2.

WHMIS CLASSIFICATION:

CLASS D, DIVISION 1, SUBDIVISION B:
TOXIC MATERIAL - ACUTE LETHALITY

CLASS D, DIVISION 2, SUBDIVISION A:

VERY TOXIC MATERIAL - CHRONIC TOXIC EFFECTS
TERATOGENICITY AND EMBRYOTOXICITY

CLASS D, DIVISION 2, SUBDIVISION B:
TOXIC MATERIAL-SKIN OR EYE IRRITATION

------SECTION 16 OTHER INFORMATION ------

NFPA RATINGS:
HEALTH: 2
FLAMMABILITY: 1
REACTIVITY: 0

HMIS RATINGS:
HEALTH: 2*
FLAMMABILITY: 1
REACTIVITY: 0

0-LEAST
1-SLIGHT
2-MODERATE
3-HIGH
4-EXTREME
PPE:- PERSONAL PROTECTION EQUIPMENT INDEX RECOMMENDATION
*-CHRONIC EFFECT INDICATOR
THESE VALUES ARE OBTAINED USING THE GUIDELINES OR PUBLISHED EVALUATIONS
PREPARED BY THE NATIONAL FIRE PROTECTION ASSOCIATION (NFPA) OR THE NATIONAL
PAINT AND COATING ASSOCIATION (FOR HMIS RAINGS).

REVISION STATEMENT:
THIS REVISION UPDATES SECTION 2 (COMPOSITION/INGREDIENT INFORMATION),
SECTION 5 (FIRE FIGHTING MEASURES), SECTION 11 (TOXICOLOGICAL INFORMATION),
AND SECTION 15 (REGULATORY INFORMATION).

ABBREVIATIONS THAT MAY HAVE BEEN USED IN THIS DOCUMENT:
TLV - THRESHOLD LIMIT VALUE
TWA - TIME WEIGHTED AVERAGE
STEL - SHORT-TERM EXPOSURE LIMIT
PEL - PERMISSIBLE EXPOSURE LIMIT
CAS - CHEMICAL ABSTRACT SERVICE NUMBER
NDA - NO DATA AVAILABLE
NA - NOT APPLICABLE
<= - LESS THAN OR EQUAL TO
>= - GREATER THAN OR EQUAL TO

PREPARED ACCORDING TO THE OSHA HAZARD COMMUNICATION STANDARD (29 CFR
1910.1200) AND THE ANSI MSDS STANDARD (Z400.1).

THE ABOVE INFORMATION IS BASED ON THE DATA OF WHICH WE ARE AWARE AND IS
BELIEVED TO BE CORRECT AS OF THE DATE HEREOF. SINCE THIS INFORMATION MAY BE
APPLIED UNDER CONDITIONS BEYOND OUR CONTROL AND WITH WHICH WE MAY BE
UNFAMILIAR AND SINCE DATA MADE AVAILABLE SUBSEQUENT TO THE DATE HEREOF MAY
SUGGEST MODIFICATIONS OF THE INFORMATION, WE DO NOT ASSUME ANY
RESPONSIBILITY FOR THE RESULTS OF ITS USE. THIS INFORMATION IS FURNISHED
UPON CONDITION THAT THE PERSON RECEIVING IT SHALL MAKE HIS OWN DETERMINATION
OF THE SUITABILITY OF THE MATERIAL FOR THIS PARTICULAR PURPOSE.

U.S. COMPLIANCE TIMELINE

Many laws and regulations govern those who use chemicals in the United States. It's easy to feel lost in the shuffle. Whether you are a CEO, a vice president of EHS, or a company representative having to consider government compliance, you may find some helpful information in the thumbnail sketches of the federal regulations with which you must comply. Meanwhile, many states have their own laws and regulations that exceed Uncle Sam's.

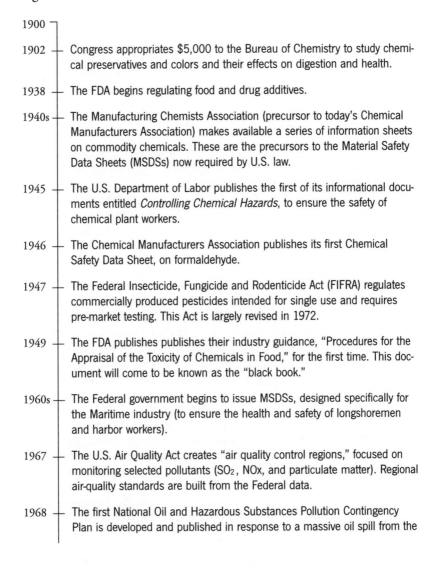

1900

1902 — Congress appropriates $5,000 to the Bureau of Chemistry to study chemical preservatives and colors and their effects on digestion and health.

1938 — The FDA begins regulating food and drug additives.

1940s — The Manufacturing Chemists Association (precursor to today's Chemical Manufacturers Association) makes available a series of information sheets on commodity chemicals. These are the precursors to the Material Safety Data Sheets (MSDSs) now required by U.S. law.

1945 — The U.S. Department of Labor publishes the first of its informational documents entitled *Controlling Chemical Hazards*, to ensure the safety of chemical plant workers.

1946 — The Chemical Manufacturers Association publishes its first Chemical Safety Data Sheet, on formaldehyde.

1947 — The Federal Insecticide, Fungicide and Rodenticide Act (FIFRA) regulates commercially produced pesticides intended for single use and requires pre-market testing. This Act is largely revised in 1972.

1949 — The FDA publishes publishes their industry guidance, "Procedures for the Appraisal of the Toxicity of Chemicals in Food," for the first time. This document will come to be known as the "black book."

1960s — The Federal government begins to issue MSDSs, designed specifically for the Maritime industry (to ensure the health and safety of longshoremen and harbor workers).

1967 — The U.S. Air Quality Act creates "air quality control regions," focused on monitoring selected pollutants (SO_2, NOx, and particulate matter). Regional air-quality standards are built from the Federal data.

1968 — The first National Oil and Hazardous Substances Pollution Contingency Plan is developed and published in response to a massive oil spill from the oil tanker *Torrey Canyon* off the coast of England the year before. More than 37 million gallons of crude oil spilled into the water, causing massive environmental damage. To avoid the problems faced by response officials involved in this incident, U.S. officials develop this coordinated approach to cope with potential spills in U.S. waters. The plan provides the first comprehensive system of accident reporting, spill containment, and cleanup, and establishes a response headquarters, a national reaction team, and regional reaction teams. The National Contingency Plan (NCP), is the federal government's blueprint for responding to both oil spills and hazardous substance releases.

1969 — The National Environmental Policy Act (NEPA) establishes the first national environmental policy and creates the Council on Environmental Quality (CEQ).

— The Federal Coal Mine Health and Safety Act is passed to protect the health and safety of the nation's coal miners.

1970 — The first U.S. "Earth Day" is held, a nationwide demonstration of support for the environment by 20 million Americans.

— The Environmental Protection Agency (EPA) is created and charged with enforcing the Clean Air Act, which amends 1967's Air Quality Act. Now the Federal government has a regulatory structure for monitoring environmental quality in the United States. The EPA, examining criteria pollutants, later creates national ambient air quality standards (NAAQS) to be used by states for creating their individual source emission limitations in state implementation plans (SIPs). The Clean Air Act amendments also regulate hazardous air pollutants and establish a special set of New Source Performance Standards.

— The Occupational Safety and Health Administration (OSHA) Act is established to ensure safe and healthful workplaces in America. (The Act creating OSHA is later amended in 1990.) OSHA creates, issues, and enforces occupational safety and health standards and regulations, issuing citations for noncompliance. The OSHA Act applies to most private employers in the U.S. with more than 10 employees. OSHA's standards for toxic and hazardous substances cover such categories as air contaminants, asbestos, lead, benzene, ionizing radiation, and hazard communication. For airborne exposure, OSHA establishes "permissible exposure limits" (PELs) to about 420 specific compounds. Employers are required to provide protection, training, information, and monitoring of employees potentially exposed to hazardous substances. The process safety management (PSM) standard is designed to prevent or minimize the consequences of catastrophic releases of toxic, reactive, flammable, and explosive chemicals. Employers covered under the PSM rule must have emergency action plans specifying procedures for reporting fires and emergencies, and for emergency response operations for releases or the threat of releases.

1971 — The EPA is busy on air quality, setting the "four corners" air quality boundaries, setting up national air quality standards, and defining air pollution danger levels.

1972 — Major revisions are made to FIFRA. FIFRA now requires that each manufacturer register each pesticide and its label with the EPA before it can be manufactured for commercial use.

— Congress mandates the Federal Water Pollution Control Act (FWPCA), and the Marine Protection, Research and Sanctuaries Act (MPRSA) of 1972. These Acts are meant to protect and restore the quality of the nation's surface waters.

— The Ocean Dumping Act is passed.

— The EPA bans DDT.

1973 — The EPA begins to take on automakers and the petroleum companies by setting auto maintenance regulations and transportation controls in major urban areas, as well as beginning a phaseout of leaded gasoline.

— The EPA issues its first wastewater permits.

1974 — OSHA adopts health standards for 14 known carcinogens.

— The Safe Drinking Water Act (SDWA) is established to protect human health from contaminants in drinking water and to prevent contamination of existing groundwater supplies.

— The EPA identifies noise levels affecting health and welfare.

— The EPA issues its "significant deterioration" regulations.

1975 — OSHA issues a generic cancer policy, declaring any material that produces tumors in animals to be a human carcinogen and requiring exposure limits to be lowered to the lowest attainable limit.

— The EPA requires working catalytic converters on imported cars.

— The federal government cuts aid to polluters.

— The EPA bans the manufacture of heptachlor and chlordane.

1976 — The Resource Conservation and Recovery Act (RCRA)—amending the old Solid Waste Disposal Act—regulates the creation, transportation, storage, treatment, and disposal of solid and hazardous wastes. RCRA addresses "cradle-to-grave" requirements for hazardous waste from the point of generation to disposal. Nonhazardous solid waste is not dealt with as severely. Hazardous waste characteristics include toxicity, corrosivity, ignitability, and reactivity.

The Toxic Substances Control Act (TSCA) gives the EPA broad authority to regulate the manufacture, use, distribution in commerce, and disposal of chemical substances. The Act goes through several major revisions in the next couple of decades. Overseen by the EPA Office of Pollution Prevention and Toxics (OPPT), TSCA requires manufacturers to perform health and environmental testing, use quality control in production processes, and notify the EPA of products' possible adverse health effects. Among the chemicals the EPA regulates under TSCA are asbestos, CFCs, and polychlorinated biphenyls (PCBs).

1977   The Clean Water Act (CWA) amends the FWPCA and adds a major program to control toxic water pollutants. (In many states environmental requirements later become more strict than federal CWA requirements.) Under the Act, it is unlawful to discharge pollutants into waterways—such as rivers, lakes, streams, and wetlands—except as provided for by the Act. Five major types of requirements that directly affect the chemical industry are point-source direct discharge limitations, pretreatment requirements for indirect discharges, storm water standards, oil and hazardous substances spill prevention and response, and wetlands modification (including dredge and fill operations).

EPA promotes scrubbers for coal-fired power plants.

Clean Air Act Amendments of 1977 passed.

1978   The Department of Transportation and EPA work together on the Hazardous Materials Transportation Act (Title 49), the purpose of which is to provide adequate protection against the risks to life and property inherent in the transportation of hazardous material in commerce.

EPA sets new a air standard for lead.

EPA bans aerosol fluorocarbons.

Great Lakes Water Quality Agreement is passed.

1979   PCB manufacturing is banned in the U.S.

The EPA institutes the Hazardous Waste Enforcement/Emergency Response System.

The EPA issues the Bubble Policy.

The U.S. sues for the Love Canal cleanup.

1980 — The Superfund (Comprehensive Environmental Response Compensation, and Liability — CERCLA) Act establishes liabilities for the owners, transporters, and generators of hazardous wastes. It also establishes a fund to help pay for cleanup. Ultimately, many states will introduce their own state-level Superfund laws which complement, and in some cases exceed, federal CERCLA requirements. By the end of the century, chemical industry will be paying some $300 million a year in Superfund chemical feedstock taxes.

1981 — The EPA identifies the first 114 top-priority Superfund sites.

— The EPA authorizes the first state hazardous waste programs.

1982 — The Asbestos School Hazard Abatement Act is passed.

1983 — OSHA issues a ruling that will require an MSDS for any hazardous material shipped by a U.S. manufacturer.

— The EPA bans EDB.

— The EPA starts its "Fishbowl Policy."

1984 — Hazardous and Solid Waste Amendments (HSWA) to RCRA establish additional waste management requirements and add "Subtitle I," imposing management requirements for underground storage tanks (USTs) that contain petroleum or hazardous substances.

1985 — The Chemical Emergency Preparedness and Prevention Office (CEPPO) is organized under the EPA to promote "the safe handling of chemicals." The CEPPO is formed in response to the 1984 chemical disaster in Bhopal, India, that killed more than 2,000 people. EPA states it has "taken a leading role in building programs to respond to and prevent chemical accidents."

— The EPA sets new limits on lead in gasoline.

— The EPA expands the air toxics program.

1986 — Establishment of the Superfund Amendments and Reauthorization Act (SARA), revising some sections of CERCLA, extends taxing authority for Superfund and creates a free-standing law, SARA Title III, also known as the Emergency Planning and Community Right-to-Know Act (EPCRA). This Act requires businesses/industries to publicly disclose chemicals and toxic hazards in their operations. EPCRA is specifically intended to improve local community access to information about chemical hazards and improve state and local emergency response capabilities. There are four types of reporting obligations for facilities that store or manage specifically listed chemicals under EPCRA: notification of extremely hazardous substances, notification during releases, emergency planning, and a toxic release inventory (called Form R reporting). A mandated separate Tier II form provides information about each specific hazardous chemical.

All U.S. manufacturers, importers, distributors, and employers who generate, transport, store, use, and/or dispose of hazardous materials are required by OSHA to have MSDS available/accessible for each separate chemical product, to ensure employees' right to know and emergency preparedness.

The Safe Drinking Water Act Amendments of 1986 passes.

The EPA commits to wetlands protection.

The Asbestos Hazard Emergency Response Act passes.

1987   The Water Quality Act passes, regulating "toxic hot spots" and storm water discharges.

The EPA mandates sanctions for states not meeting air standards.

Hazardous chemical reporting rule passes.

The EPA authorizes thermal destruction of dioxin at Love Canal.

1988   The EPA sets standards for underground storage tanks.

The FIFRA Amendments of 1988 are passed.

Indoor Radon Abatement Act is passed.

The Ocean Dumping Ban Act is passed.

1989   The EPA publishes first Toxic Release Inventory (TRI).

The EPA begins to track medical wastes.

Daminozide (Alar) is banned for food uses.

1990   The Pollution Prevention Act (PPA) extends reporting requirements (under EPCRA) for releases of toxic chemicals and reporting about source reduction and recycling activities related to those chemical releases. PPA also calls for a national effort to prevent or reduce pollution at the source, recycle, and treat pollution in an environmentally safe manner. Under the Act, "disposal or other release of pollution into the environment should be employed only as a last resort and should be conducted in an environmentally safe manner."

The Oil Pollution Act of 1990 tightens controls on discharges of oil and other hazardous substances. This Act is signed into law by President George Bush, after several large oil spills, including the notorious *Exxon Valdez* oil tanker spill in Alaska.

Major amendments to the Clean Air Act significantly alter regulation of hazardous air pollutants. The amendments also contain new requirements on ambient air quality and mobile source emissions, establish a new operating permit program, and set new controls on electric utility emissions of SO_2 and NO_x and substances that deplete stratospheric ozone.

The EPA's Risk Management Program Rule (RMP Rule) requires companies of all sizes that use certain flammable and toxic substances ("extremely hazardous substances") to develop a Risk Management Program for chemical accident prevention. The Risk Management Program is about reducing chemical risk at the local level. This information helps local fire, police, and emergency response personnel (who must prepare for and respond to chemical accidents) and is useful to citizens in understanding the chemical hazards in communities.

EPA restricts the land disposal of hazardous waste.

The EPA Science Advisory Board recommends its environmental risk reduction strategy.

1991 — The acid rain emission sales rule is passed.

The EPA establishes its voluntary toxics reduction program.

The federal recycling order is signed.

1992 — The EPA issues final drinking water standards for 23 chemicals.

The EPA commits to reducing environmental risks to minorities.

1993 — The EPA designates passive smoke a human carcinogen.

The sulfur dioxide trading rule is passed.

Federal facilities are ordered to reduce toxic emissions.

The EPA requires full phaseout of CFCs and other polluting elements that deplete the earth's ozone layer.

1994 — More than 300 additional chemicals are added to the list of chemicals for which reporting is required under EPCRA. The EPA also issues a citizen right-to-know list of toxics.

Chemical industry air toxics reduction rule passes.

OSHA's proposal on indoor air quality (i.e., second-hand smoke from cigarettes) evokes the largest public response in the agency's history, with more the 100,000 comments received when the comment period closes in the fall of 1995. The post-hearing comment period ends in early 1996, though the agency will eventually withdraw its indoor air quality proposal and terminate its rulemaking process in 2001. (By that time, many U.S. business owners will have already banned workplace smoking.)

1995 — The EPA initiates the Partnership for Safe Water.

— The EPA expands acid rain emissions trading.

— Refinery air toxics rule passes.

— The U.S. commits to monitoring the environment using remote-sensing data.

1996 — The Food Quality Protection Act of 1996 features revisions to FIFRA.

— The Safe Drinking Water Act Amendments of 1996 are passed.

— The EPA finalizes the leaded gas ban, affecting automakers from here on out.

— The EPA approves first Project XL plan.

— The EPA implements lead-based paint right-to-know.

1997 — The EPA implements the Food Quality Protection Act.

— U.S. and Canada move to eliminate toxics in the Great Lakes.

— The EPA website provides access to watershed data.

1998 — Emergency Planning and Community Right to Know; Section 313, Toxic Release Inventory Reporting — Receipt of Petition to Add Airports (SIC 45) (63 FR 6691) passes.

— Federal Clean Water Action Plan issued.

— The EPA website provides access to local pollution data.

1999 — The EPA lowers reporting thresholds for certain Persistent Bioaccumulative Toxic (PBT) chemicals.

— Superfund Reform accelerates hazardous waste cleanups.

2000 — The EPA endorses a cleaner diesel fuels plan.

— The EPA bans most Dursban uses.

— The EPA proposes Hudson River PCBs cleanup plan, after the GE Hudson Falls Plant discharged PCBs into New York's Hudson River.

2001 — The U.S. signs the Convention on Persistent Organic Pollutants.

2002 — The EPA awards Brownfields grants to assess the contamination of abandoned properties.

— The EPA issues the Strategic Plan for Homeland Security.

BETTER CHEMICAL MANAGEMENT
REFERENCES

Books

Baily, Ronald, ed. *Earth Report 2000: Revisiting the True State of the Planet.* New York: McGraw-Hill, 2000.

Beder, Sharon. *Global Spin: The Corporate Assault on Environmentalism.* White River Junction, VT: Green Books, 1997.

Bierma, Thomas J., Francis L. Waterstraat Jr. *Chemical Management: Reducing Waste and Cost Through Innovative Supply Strategies.* New York: John Wiley & Sons, 2000.

Cairncross, Frances. *Green, Inc.: A Guide to Business and the Environment.* Washington DC: Island Press, 1995.

Citrin, James M., Paul B. Brown and Jason Baumgarten. *Zoom: How 12 Exceptional Companies Are Navigating the Road to the Next Economy.* New York: Currency Doubleday, 2002.

Collins, Jim. *Good to Great: Why Some Companies Make the Leap…and Others Don't.* New York: HarperBusiness, 2001.

Denton, D. Keith. *Enviro-Management: How Smart Companies Turn Environmental Costs into Profits.* Englewood Cliffs: Prentice Hall, 1994.

Fagin, Dan, et al. *Toxic Deception: How the Chemical Industry Manipulates Science, Bends the Law, and Endangers Your Health.* Secaucus, NJ: Birch Lane Press, 1996.

Freeman, Edward, Jessica Pierce, and Richard H. Dodd. *Environmentalism and the New Logic of Business: How Firms Can Be Profitable and Leave Our Children a Living Planet.* Oxford: Oxford University Press, 2000.

Garten, Jeffery E. *The Mind of the C.E.O.* New York: Perseus Publishing, 2001.

Goetsch, David L. *Implementing Total Safety Management: Safety, Health, and Competitiveness in the Global Marketplace.* Upper Saddle River, NJ: Prentice Hall, 1998.

Harvard Business Review on Business and the Environment. Cambridge: Harvard Business School Press, 2000.

Karliner, Joshua. *The Corporate Planet: Ecology and Politics in the Age of Globalization.* San Francisco: Sierra Club Books, 1997.

Kerzner, Harold. *In Search of Excellence in Project Management: Successful Practices in High Performance Organizations.* New York: Van Nostrand Reinhold, 1998.

Kinlaw, Dennis C. *Competitive & Green: Sustainable Performance in the Environmental Age.* San Diego: Pfeiffer Press, 1993.

Koop, C. Everett, Clarence E. Pearson, and M. Roy Schwarz. *Critical Issues in Global Health*. San Francisco: Jossey-Bass, 2002.

LaDou, Joseph, ed. *Occupational Health & Safety*, 2nd Edition. Itasca, IL: National Safety Council, 1994.

Manning, Michael V. *"So, You're the Safety Director!" An Introduction to Loss Control and Safety Management*. Rockville, MD: Government Institutes, 1998.

McInerny, Francis, and Sean White. *The Total Quality Corporation: How 10 Major Companies Turned Quality and Environmental Challenges to Competitive Advantage in the 1990s*. New York: Truman Talley Books/Dutton, 1995.

Monks, Robert A. G., and Nell Minow. *Power and Accountability*. New York: HarperBusiness, 1991.

Nattrass, Brian, and Mary Altomare. *The Natural Step for Business: Wealth, Ecology and the Evolutionary Corporation*. British Columbia: New Society Publishers, 1999.

Peters, Tom. *The Circle of Innovation: You Can't Shrink Your Way to Greatness*. New York: Alfred A. Knopf, 1997.

Petersen, Dan. *Analyzing Safety System Effectiveness*. New York: Van Nostrand Reinhold, 1996.

Piasecki, Bruce W. *Corporate Environmental Strategy: The Avalanche of Change Since Bhopal*. New York: John Wiley & Sons, 1995.

Richards, Deanna J., ed. *Industrial Green Game: Implications for Environmental Design and Management*. Washington DC: National Academy Press, 1997.

Saunders, Tedd. *The Bottom Line of Green is Black*. San Francisco: HarperSanFrancisco, 1993.

Sayre, Don. *Inside ISO 14000: The Competitive Advantage of Environmental Management*. Delray Beach, FL: St. Lucie Press, 1996.

Schell, David J. *A Green Plan for Industry: 16 Steps to Environmental Excellence*. Rockville, MD: Government Institutes, 1998.

Sullivan, Thomas F. P., ed. *The Greening of American Business: Making Bottom-Line Sense of Environmental Responsibility*. Rockville, MD: Government Institutes, 1992.

Taylor, Graham D., and Patricia Sudnik. *DuPont and the International Chemical Industry*. Boston: Twayne Publishers, 1984.

Magazines, Reports, and Websites

"Facts and Figures for the Chemical Industry." *CENEAR* vol. 80, no. 25. (2002) American Chemical Society Website: http://pubs.acs.org/cen

"US Chemical Industry." American Chemistry Council Website: http://www.americanchemistry.com

Burns, Paul. "Multi-stakeholder Success Stories: Toxics Use Reduction in Massachusetts, USA." October 2000. World Wildlife Organization Website: http://www.worldwildlife.org/toxics/pubres/massachusetts.pdf

"BSR White Papers: Accountability." Business for Social Responsibility Website: http://www.bsr.org

"Sustainable Growth 2001 Progress Report." DuPont Website: http://www.dupont.com/corp/social/SHE/index.html

"What Makes One Chemical More Hazardous than Another?" 2002. Ecolink Website: http://www.ecolink.com/cleanideas/toxicred.html

Ember, Lois R. "Science in the Service of Security." *CENEAR* vol. 80, no. 49. December 2002. American Chemical Society Website: http://pubs.acs.org/cen/coverstory/8049/print/8049homeland.html

"Waste Minimization Fact Sheets." Environment Canada Website: http://www.ns.ec.gc.ca/epb/pollprev/wm_factsheets/chemfs.html

"EPA Announces Homeland Security Strategic Plan, One of Many Efforts to Ensure Agency's Ability to Protect, Respond and Recover." 22 October 2002. EPA Website: http://www.epa.gov/epahome/headline_100202.htm

EnviroSense. "The Massachusetts Toxics Use Reduction Institute: Toxics Use Reduction, Fact Sheet 1: What is Toxics Use Reduction?" EPA Website: http://es.epa.gov/techinfo/facts/mass/tura-fs1.html

Fisher, Jim. "Poison Valley: Is Workers' Health the Price We Pay for High Tech Progress?" *Salon*, 30 July 2001. Salon Website: http://dir.salon.com/tech/feature/2001/07/30/almaden1/index.html

Global Environmental Management Initiative Website: http://www.gemi.org

"Corporate Responsibility, Policies and Performance." Merck Website: http://www.merck.com/about/cr/policies_performance/environmental/policy.html

"Index of Leading Environmental Indicators, 2000: Sustainable Development." Pacific Research Institute Website: http://www.pacificresearch.org/pub/sab/enviro/00_enviroindex/sustain.html

Hayward, Steven F., and Julie Majeres. "Index of Leading Environmental Indicators 7th Edition." San Francisco: Pacific Research Institute, April 2002. Pacific Research Institute Website: http://www.pacificresearch.org/pub/sab/enviro/ei2002-states/pri_enviro_index_2002.pdf

Hayward, Steven, and Ryan Stowers. "Index of Leading Environmental Indicators 8th Edition." San Francisco: Pacific Research Institute, April 2003. Pacific Research Institute Website: http://www.pacificresearch.org/pub/sab/enviro/03_enviroindex/ei_03_cover.pdf

"Toxics Release Inventory and Pesticides." Pacific Research Institute Website: http://www.pacificresearch.org/pub/sab/enviro/01_enviroindex/toxics.html

Sierra Club. "Sierra Club Urges Senators to Approve Treaty to Eliminate Toxic Chemicals, Protect Public Health." *San Diego Earth Times*, June 2002. San Diego Earth Times Website: http://www.sdearthtimes.com/et0602/et0602s12.html

"Texas Instruments Lead-Free Solutions." Texas Instruments Website: http://www.ti.com/sc/docs/products/leadfree/legislation.htm

"What is Toxics Use Reduction?" Toxics Use Reduction Institute Website: http://www.turi.org/HTMLSrc/TUR.html

United States Department of Labor. "National Census of Fatal Occupational Injuries in 2000." 14 August 2002. U.S. Bureau of Labor Statistics Website: http://stats.bls.gov/oshhome.htm

United States Department of Labor. "Safety and Health Topics: Homeland Security in the Workplace – Bioterrorism." 12 December 2002. Occupational Safety and Health Administration Website: http://www.osha.gov/SLTC/biologicalagents/bioterrorism.html

United States General Accounting Office. *Environmental Protection: EPA Should Strengthen Its Efforts to Measure and Encourage Pollution Prevention.* Report to Congressional Requesters, February 2001.

Votta, Tom. "Achieving Chemical Use Reduction and Waste Minimization through the Chemical Supply Chain." RCRA National Meeting, Washington, D.C., 15 January 2002. Chemical Strategies Partnership Website: http://www.chemicalstrageties.org

Walsh, Kerri. "Billion-Dollar Club: The New Lineup." *Chemical Week*. 4 December 2002: 25-38.

Wayland, Susan H. "Pollution Prevention: Some Thoughts from the US EPA." National Pollution Prevention Roundtable. Hyatt Regency Capitol Hill Hotel, Washington, DC, April 9, 1999. EPA Website: http://www.epa.gov/oppt/library/archive/oppts_speeches/web299fw.htm

Westervelt, Robert. "ACC Forecasts Stronger Growth in 2003." *Chemical Week*. 4 December 2002.

World Business Council for Sustainable Development. "Environmental Performance and Shareholder Value." 1995.

GLOSSARY

Application Service Provider (ASP): computer-data applications provided as a service, instead of as licensed software installed and used at the client's facility. ASPs are frequently web based and may include downloadable software (in Java) and remote-disk storage solutions.

Bureau of Labor Statistics (BLS): the main U.S. federal government agency data source for national information and statistics relevant to social and economic conditions pertinent to workers, workplaces, and workers' families.

chemical life cycle: the entire spectrum of human health, environmental and financial costs, and liabilities surrounding the procurement, storage, use, and disposal of chemicals. When companies consider chemical life cycles that look beyond the mere initial purchase price of the products, a better picture of total chemical costs may be obtained.

civil action: a formal lawsuit, filed in court, against a person who has either failed to comply with a statutory or regulatory requirement or an administrative order, or a lawsuit against a person who has contributed to a release of hazardous waste/constituents.

Clean Air Act (CAA): the federal act that regulates air emissions from area, stationary, and mobile sources. CAA limits the emission of pollutants into the atmosphere in order to protect human health and the environment from the effects of airborne pollution.

Clean Water Act (CWA): the federal act that sets the basic structure for regulating discharges of pollutants into surface waters of the United States. CWA imposes contaminant limitations or guidelines for all discharges of wastewater into the nation's waterways.

Compliance-Side Total Chemical Management (CSTCM): a process for improving chemical procurement decisions to reduce the number and volume of chemicals used by business and industry, and to increase human, environmental and fiscal health. CSTCM works through the existing EHS/government compliance departments already in place at many companies.

Comprehensive Environmental Response, Compensation, and Liability Act (CERCLA): the act that authorizes the EPA to clean up uncontrolled or abandoned hazardous waste sites and respond to accidents, spills, and other emergency releases of hazardous substances. CERCLA provides the EPA with enforcement authority to ensure that responsible parties pay the cleanup costs of improving a site contaminated with hazardous substances.

corporate responsibility (and sustainability): an ethics-based business attitude that has been driven by socially conscious consumers, workers, investors, politicians, and business leaders in the latter half of the 20th and early 21st centuries. Corporate responsibility dictates that business leaders consider values and ensure their companies are accountable for implementing and acting upon socially, environmentally, and financially responsible policies and practices. Brand enhancement and increased market share are possible dividends of corporate responsibility.

cradle-to-grave: the time period referring to the initial generation of hazardous waste to its ultimate disposal.

disposal: the discharge, deposit, injection, dumping, spilling, leaking, or placing of any liquid, gaseous, or solid hazardous waste on or in the land or water.

Emergency Planning and Community Right-to-Know Act (EPCRA): the act designed to help communities prepare to respond in the event of a chemical emergency, and to increase the public's knowledge of the presence and threat of hazardous chemicals. This is the EPA's so-called SARA Title III regulatory element, enacted by Congress, and requires companies to report their hazardous chemical inventories annually to local and state emergency planning organizations and first responders.

Environmental Health and Safety (EHS): that area of a business responsible for making sure a company is aware of and adheres to all applicable environmental and safety-related compliance requirements. The EHS manager, or other department head, is often responsible for emergency response planning, training, drills, monitoring, and reporting and the mitigation of releases of hazardous materials to the environment. The EHS manager often is also the individual responsible for maintaining access to the company's MSDSs.

Environmental Protection Agency (EPA): the federal agency responsible for protecting human health and safeguarding the natural environment—defined as the air, water, and land. The EPA works with other federal agencies, state and local governments, and Indian tribes to develop and enforce regulations under existing environmental laws. The EPA is responsible for researching and setting national standards for a variety of environmental programs, delegates to states and tribes responsibility for issuing permits, and monitors and enforces compliance. Where national standards are not met, the EPA can issue sanctions and take other steps to assist the states and tribes in reaching the desired levels of environmental quality. The agency also works with industries and all levels of government in a wide variety of voluntary pollution prevention programs and energy conservation efforts. The agency employs about 18,000 people in its Washington, D.C. headquarters, 10 regional offices, and more than one dozen laboratories nationwide. The EPA hosts an outstanding, searchable website—http://www.epa.gov—which can give you information on all the laws and regulations applicable to any company that deals with chemicals.

Enterprise Resource Planning (ERP) system: an integrated software solution used to manage all or most of a company's resources, such as planning, inventory and materials management, engineering, order processing, manufacturing, purchasing, accounting and finance, and human resources. Major ERP providers include SAP, PeopleSoft, and Oracle.

Extremely Hazardous Substances (EHS): refers to substances regulated under SARA Section 302, which are particularly hazardous and have lower reporting thresholds.

Federal Insecticide, Fungicide and Rodenticide Act (FIFRA): the act that provides procedures for the registration of pesticide products to control their introduction into the marketplace.

formal action: an enforcement action, frequently in the form of an administrative order, which is taken when a serious violation is detected or when the owner and operator does not respond to an informal administrative action.

Form R: a form required by EPCRA that the owner or operator of regulated facilities must submit to the EPA and the state in which a plant is located, summarizing the releases of each toxic chemical at the facility during the preceding calendar year.

Government Accounting Office (GAO): appointed by Congress, this organization studies the programs and expenditures of the federal government. Often referred to as the investigative "watchdog" of Congress, the GAO is independent and nonpartisan. It studies how the federal government spends taxpayer dollars. The GAO advises Congress and the heads of executive agencies (such as the EPA, Department of Defense, and Department of Health and Human Services) about ways to make government more effective and responsive. The GAO evaluates federal programs, audits federal expenditures, and issues legal opinions. When the GAO reports its findings to Congress, it recommends actions. Its work contributes to laws and acts meant to improve government operations and save the government money.

hazard: according to the EPA, a substance exhibiting 1) the potential for radiation, a chemical, or other pollutant to cause human illness or injury, and 2) in the pesticide program, the inherent toxicity of a compound. Hazard identification of a given substance is an informed judgment based on verifiable toxicity data from animal models or human studies.

hazardous chemical: as defined by the Hazard Communication Standard (HCS), a hazardous chemical is one that can cause a physical or health hazard. The chemical manufacturer makes the determination. Chemical manufacturers are not required to provide MSDSs for chemicals not covered under the HCS.

HAZCOM (Hazard Communication): refers to "hazard communication" under OSHA's Hazard Communication Standard (HCS). OSHA has estimated that more than 32 million workers are exposed to 650,000 hazardous chemical products in more than 3 million American workplaces. The basic goal of a Hazard Communication Program is to be sure employers and employees know about work hazards and how to protect themselves.

Hazard Communication Standard (HCS) 29 CFR 1910.1200: requires employers to establish Hazard Communication Programs to transmit information on the hazards of chemicals to their employees by means of labels on containers, MSDSs, and training programs. Implementation of these hazard communication programs will ensure all employees have the right to know the hazards and identities of the chemicals they work with, and will reduce the incidence of chemically-related occupational illnesses and injuries. Besides containing other important data, the HCS specifies the required information that must be on each MSDS.

hazardous waste: waste with properties that make it dangerous or capable of having a harmful effect on human health and the environment. Hazardous wastes may refer to liquids, solids, or gas, or may (under RCRA) be solids. Wastes are considered hazardous if they exhibit any one of the four hazardous waste characteristics (ignitability, corrosivity, reactivity, or toxicity). Essentially, wastes are hazardous under the definition of the law if, 1) they are listed (specifically named), or 2) if they exhibit any of mixtures of a solid waste and a listed hazardous waste. A formal definition of hazardous wastes can be found in 40 CFR 261.3.

hurdle rate: the required rate of return in a discounted cash flow analysis, above which an investment makes sense and below which it does not. This is often based on the firm's cost of capital or weighted average cost of capital, plus or minus a risk premium to reflect the project's specific risk characteristics. This is also called "required rate of return."

integrated management (IM): a continuous, dynamic style of managing corporate resources in which decisions are made for the sustainable development and improvement of the whole company. In order to overcome the fragmentation that exists in less robust management styles, IM analyzes and addresses conflicting interdepartmental issues and promotes harmonizing linkages and activities in order to serve a greater corporate goal.

inventory integration: a method, usually software-based, by which chemical inventories may be tracked, compared, and streamlined concerning on-hand and on-order quantities/volumes, as well as committed and available quantities/volumes. May include data on varying job status and transfers and use of chemicals between locations.

life-cycle costing: any one of various methods for determining the total cost of ownership of chemicals in a business operation over the life of the chemical product. This would include the chemical's cost (purchase price), as well as the cost of chemical handling, storage, disposal, and any applicable risk-management issues related to the product.

material request and approval: the process by which necessary chemicals are identified, ordered, and procured within an individual company.

MSDS (Material Safety Data Sheet): a hazardous-chemical-specific document designed to provide U.S. workers and emergency personnel with the proper procedures for handling or working with a particular substance. Chemical manufacturers are required to provide a separate MSDS for each chemical product covered under OSHA's HCS. At the time of publication, there were literally millions of MSDSs in existence. MSDSs include product-specific information such as physical reactivity data (melting point, boiling point, flash point, etc.), toxicity, health effects, and appropriate first aid, storage, disposal, protective equipment, and spill/leak procedures. This data is of particular use if a spill, accident, or exposure occurs. The information in MSDSs helps companies comply with federal and state regulations, such as OSHA's HCS. MSDSs are also valuable for companies that must comply with the EPA's Community Right-to-Know Law (SARA Title III). Individual states also require companies in their jurisdictions to maintain MSDSs. There is no official format for MSDSs in the U.S., though OSHA has a suggested format (Form 174) and prefers that companies use an ANSI format.

National Ambient Air Quality Standards: regulations promulgated by the EPA under the Clean Air Act for six criteria pollutants, including: sulfur dioxide, particulate matter, nitrogen dioxide, carbon monoxide, ozone, and lead. The purpose of the standards is to protect the public from toxic emissions into the atmosphere.

National Emission Standards for Hazardous Air Pollutants: standards set by the EPA under the Clean Air Act to control emissions from specific industrial sources.

Nontoxic CEO: a company leader who reduces where possible and responsibly manages hazardous chemicals at all times for the greater protection of people, the planet, and profits.

Occupational Safety and Health Administration (OSHA): the federal agency responsible for preventing work-related injuries, illnesses, and deaths. Since OSHA was created in 1971, the agency reports it has reduced occupational injuries by 40 percent and deaths by 50 percent. With its resources bolstered by 26 state-related agencies, OSHA employees conducted nearly 97,000 workplace inspections in 2002. The agency levies fines up to $70,000 for violations of standards under the OSHA Act. OSHA reports that it prioritizes its mission as follows (in descending order of importance): reports of imminent dangers/accidents about to happen; fatalities or accidents serious enough to send three or more workers to the hospital; employee complaints; referrals from other government agencies; targeted inspections, such as the Site Specific Targeting Program, which focuses on employers that report high injury and illness rates. Follow-up inspections are the final agency priority. OSHA's Hazardous Communication Standard requires chemical manufacturers to provide a separate MSDS for each chemical product that the agency deems hazardous. General OSHA health and safety standards are available by searching 29 CRF 1910 on the OSHA website—http://www.osha.gov. Standards for toxic/hazardous substances are in Subpart Z of the citation. OSHA's website also provides standards for hazardous waste, airborne permissible exposure limits, and process safety management.

P-card (purchase card): an alternative to purchase orders and out-of-pocket expenses for authorized company employees. P-cards operate similarly to credit cards at merchant locations and are linked directly to corporate departments, allowing for more location-specific administrative control. P-cards usually eliminate the need to prepare payment requests forms, but because they allow vendor payments at the point of sale, chemical purchases (and considerations of potential product redundancies and hazards) are more difficult to track at a corporate enterprise-wide level.

point source discharges: discharges of treated wastewater directly into a lake, river, stream, or other water body. Point source discharges are regulated under CWA.

pollutants (contaminants): any element, substance, compound, or mixture that, after release into the environment and upon exposure, ingestion, inhalation, or assimilation into any organism, will or may reasonably be anticipated to cause illness, death, or deformation.

Pollution Prevention Act: the Pollution Prevention Act (42 U.S.C. 13101 and 13102, s/s et seq.) focused industry, government, and public attention on reducing the amount of pollution in the United States through cost-effective changes in production, operation, and raw materials use. The EPA has developed and implemented strategies to promote source reduction, including establishing standard methods of measurement of source. The EPA fosters the exchange of information regarding source reduction techniques and disseminates such information, provides technical assistance to businesses, and administers annual awards programs to recognize companies which operate outstanding or innovative source reduction programs.

regulated community: the group of organizations, people, industries, businesses, and agencies that, because they perform certain activities, fall under the purview of a regulatory agency acts.

Resource Conservation and Recovery Act (RCRA): establishes a framework for national programs to achieve environmentally sound management of both hazardous and nonhazardous wastes. The RCRA also promotes resource recovery techniques and methods to reduce the generation of hazardous waste. The RCRA is designed to protect human health and the environment, reduce/ eliminate the generation of hazardous wastes, and conserve energy and natural resources. The Hazardous and Solid Waste Amendments (HSWA) of 1984 both expanded the scope of RCRA and increased the level of detail in many of its provisions.

Right to Know: refers to each American worker's right to know about the hazards that chemicals in the workplace pose, as described in OSHA's Hazard Communication Standard.

risk-based decision making: a process that uses risk and exposure assessment concepts to help business leaders whose companies deal with chemicals make critical decisions and set priorities.

Safe Drinking Water Act: the act designed to protect the nation's drinking water supply by establishing national drinking water standards.

source reduction: maximizing or reducing the use of natural resources at the beginning of an industrial process, thereby eliminating the amount of waste produced by the process. Source reduction is the EPA's preferred method of waste management.

Superfund: the common name for CERCLA. Superfund refers to the entire CERCLA program as well as the trust fund established to fund cleanup of contaminated sites where potentially responsible parties cannot be identified, or are unwilling or unable to pay.

Superfund Amendments and Reauthorization Act (SARA): SARA, enacted in 1986, reauthorized and amended CERCLA to include additional enforcement authorities, technical requirements, community involvement requirements, and various clarifications. SARA Title III authorized EPCRA.

Supply-Side Total Chemical Management (SSTCM): a process of reducing the volume and number of chemicals and better managing them through cooperation between a company and its chemical product suppliers (vendors).

threshold: as defined by the EPA as, 1) the lowest dose of a chemical at which a specified measurable effect is observed and below which it is not observed, and 2) the dose or exposure level below which a significant adverse effect is not expected.

Tier I: the federal Superfund Program classification of a site if a release from the site has caused, or is likely to cause, human exposure to the release or contamination of a sensitive environment, and the release can be addressed under CERCLA authorities, and cleanup of the release has not been generally deferred to another Federal cleanup program. This includes, but is not limited to, sites where, 1) drinking water supplies have been, or are likely to become, contaminated with a hazardous substance (as defined in HRS), 2) soil on or in close proximity to school, day care center, or residential properties have been contaminated by a hazardous substance three times above background levels, 3) toxic substances that bioaccumulate have been discharged into surface waters, 4) air releases of hazardous substances have been identified in a populated area, 5) sensitive environments have been contaminated, or 6) releases would require immediate action from EPA (e.g., fire, explosions).

Tier II: EPA chemical-reporting forms requiring basic information about the reporting location, emergency contacts, and information about chemicals stored or used at the facility. These forms are required under Title III, Sections 311 and 312, of SARA. Some states also require additional information. Tier II sites are those that would be unlikely to warrant Federal remedial actions, i.e., those that do not meet the definition for Tier I sites. Tier II sites would also include sites that score below 28.5, based on the Hazard Ranking System (HRS), 55 FR 51532, and do not meet any of the characteristics of Tier I sites identified above. The majority of sites brought to the EPA's attention over the course of the Superfund program have scored below 28.5 and are considered Tier II.

Title III: (see also EPCRA). The EPA's consolidated list of chemicals subject to the EPCRA and Section 112(r) of the Clean Air Act (also known as the List of Lists), prepared to help firms handling chemicals determine whether they need to submit reports under sections 302, 304, or 313 of EPCRA and, for a specific chemical, what reports may need to be submitted. It also helps firms determine whether they will be subject to accident prevention regulations under CAA section 112(r). These lists should be used as a reference tool, not as a definitive source of compliance information. Compliance information for EPCRA is published in the Code of Federal Regulations (CFR), 40 CFR Parts 302, 355, and 372. Compliance information for CAA section 112(r) is published in 40 CFR Part 68. The List of Lists is available in PDF, Excel, or a searchable database that offers the user several search options. (See the EPA's website, http://www.epa.gov for more information.)

Total Chemical Management (TCM): the conscious and responsible corporate management of chemicals by way of life-cycle costing throughout the chemical life cycle (see related terms).

toxic chemical: any chemical listed in EPA rules as "Toxic Chemicals Subject to Section 313 of the Emergency Planning and Community Right-to-Know Act of 1986."

Toxic Release Inventory (TRI): a database of toxic releases in the United States compiled from SARA Title III Section 313 reports. The TRI is available to anyone on the EPA's official website.

toxic substance: a chemical or mixture that may present an unreasonable risk of injury to health or the environment.

toxic waste: a waste that can produce injury if inhaled, swallowed, or absorbed through the skin.

toxicity: the degree to which a substance or mixture of substances can harm humans or animals. Acute toxicity involves harmful effects in an organism through a single or short-term exposure. Chronic toxicity is the ability of a substance or mixture of substances to cause harmful effects over an extended period, usually upon repeated or continuous exposure, sometimes lasting for the entire life of the exposed organism. Subchronic toxicity is the ability of the substance to cause effects for more than one year but less than the lifetime of the exposed organism.